PROGRAMMING CONCEPTS IN
JAVA

ROBERT BURNS

Library of Congress Control Number:		2014919932
ISBN:	Hardcover	978-1-5035-1150-7
	Softcover	978-1-5035-1151-4
	eBook	978-1-5035-1149-1

Rev. date: 11/25/2014

To order additional copies of this book, contact:
Xlibris
1-888-795-4274
www.Xlibris.com
Orders@Xlibris.com
626895

Introduction

Computers are great! You give them "input" and they produce "output". Whether it's typing an Internet address and then seeing a web page with the latest news, or entering tax information and then printing a 1040 form with all supporting documents, or using an app on a smart phone to pay for your coffee, computers offer various ways for us to specify input and they have a variety of different ways to express their output.

Computers are fast and accurate. Humans, by comparison are slow and, let's face it, we make mistakes. Have you ever added the same list of numbers twice and gotten two different totals? But humans have something that computers do not – *intelligence*.

Computers did not design the Internet, nor did they devise the tax code. Computers did not design how smart phone touch screens work. It's the humans who figured out all of that. Somewhere along the line, a human must have *explained* to a computer just exactly what to do with the input in order to turn it into output. A human had to tell the computer how to decide if a password is valid or not. A human had to explain how to calculate amortization. A human had to define the "pinch" motion and decide how it should zoom out on a photo. Same for the "shake" motion that shuffles songs in an MP3 player.

So it's the *human+computer team* that makes all of this work. Using their intelligence, the humans have the ideas and figure out "recipes" for converting input into output. Using their speed and accuracy, the computers faithfully and reliably perform the conversions.

The humans on such teams are called "programmers". The purpose of this book is to turn *you* into a programmer.

About This Book

This book is organized into three "parts", separated by major milestones in gaining programming knowledge.

Part 1 shows how to apply basic concepts of programming. It goes through the details of writing programs using freely available "editor" and "compiler" software. It shows how to store data in "variables" for use in calculations, and how to produce nice-looking output. These chapters teach all that is needed to create simple interactive programs that gather "input", perform calculations based on the input, and display "output" using calculated results.

Part 2 adds elements of logic to the simple programs of part 1. Ways are presented for making programs selectively use different sets of instructions, based on circumstances. Ways to get a program to repeat itself are also presented, allowing things to be done more than once without duplicating the steps. These chapters teach what is needed to create more sophisticated programs with "branching" and "looping" logic, such as would be required for computer games and almost every other useful program.

Part 3 introduces the powerful concept of single variables that can store multiple values all at the same time. "Array" variables can store multiple values of the same type, and are suitable for dealing with lists, such as lists of test scores, high temperatures, or names of students. "Object" variables can store multiple values of related information, and are suitable for dealing with data records, such as student accounts with names, IDs, and addresses. Chapters 13-15 introduce advanced applications of arrays and objects, for the purpose of first exposure to some advanced computer science concepts, but primarily to provide an opportunity to apply the language elements learned in parts 1 and 2.

The **Appendix** contains excerpts from the Java "library" with references to all of the library elements used in this book. There is also an **Index** at the end.

Unique Features Of This Book

Unlike many of today's introductory textbooks, this book does *not* jump into **object-oriented programming** right away. Objects are introduced and used, particularly for such language features as input/output. Objects that encapsulate data are presented as variables that store multiple values at the same time. But a development of objects that encapsulate data *and code* and interact with other objects is specifically avoided. Instead, the focus is on the fundamental concepts of data, statements, expressions, and flow of control. These need to be well-understood in order to be used in the programming of classes and objects anyway, so rather than make the student pick up both concepts at once, full treatment of objects is left for another, later level of study.

Emphasis is on **command-line compiling** instead of IDEs, because it is a lowest common denominator of programming. In this way, Java program development is consistent among different systems such as PCs, Macs, and UNIX/Linux. But just about any IDE can be can be used in following this book, if that is the instructor's or student's choice. But because an IDE usually combines the editing and compiling steps into a single program, it's likely that the unique separation of these programming steps will be lost on the beginning student. Command-line compiling makes the student more aware of the files and folders used on the host system, and differences among operating systems become not so great.

This book makes a distinction between **expressions** and **statements**. Expressions are the building blocks of statements, and as such, they individually and separately resolve to simple values that get substituted in full statements. They are likened to "phrases" in the spoken language. Language elements that are expressions are specifically pointed out as such, and are specially notated – for example, x + y. Full statements, usually ending in a semicolon, are likened to "sentences" in the spoken language. They are notated like this: x = 1; .

This book refers to **subprograms** as "functions". In many Java references, and in its official online documentation itself,

7

subprograms are called "methods". But this book is not really intended as a Java textbook so much as it is a programming concepts textbook, and *concepts* are language-independent. So to be consistent with this book's effort to avoid language-specific terminology for generic concepts, we're going with "function", which is what they are called in C, C++, Javascript, PHP, Python, and others.

It may be surprising to see **linked lists, collections, and recursion** addressed in the later chapters. But the purpose is *not* to make the student proficient in the use or understanding of these concepts. Rather it is to provide a vehicle for practicing what was learned about variables, branching, loops, functions, arrays, and objects. And in so doing, the student is also introduced to ideas that will reappear in future studies in computer science, and be better prepared to learn them at that time.

This book is available in both **e-book and printed formats**, and supported by online publication of coding examples, sample assignments, and instructional how-to videos. URLs and links appear at the ends of chapters 1-14, where one might normally expect to find review questions and exercises. Go to www.rdb3.com/java/ebook for tips on navigating the e-book.

The language of the book is **common English** so as to keep it as approachable for students as possible. That's while you'll see contractions and exclamation marks!

Unique Java Coding Features

A peculiar expression is used in the Java console and text file input. It's:

```
new Double(cin.readLine()).intValue()
```

...for the input of "int" values. It may seem odd to refer to the "Double" class, but it allows whole numbers to be entered with a decimal point and trailing decimal digits without causing a number formatting exception.

Table of Contents

Introduction 5
    About This Book 6
    Unique Features Of This Book................................. 7
    Unique Java Coding Features 8

PART 1: The Basics 13

Chapter 1. Programming Concepts................... 15
    1.1 The First Step, Understanding............................ 15
    1.2 Editors... 16
    1.3 Compilers 18
    1.4 Elements Of Computer Languages 18
    1.5 Exercises, Sample Code, Videos, And Addendums............... 23

Chapter 2. Editing And Compiling 25
    2.1 Choosing An Editor 25
    2.2 Choosing A Compiler 28
    2.3 Choosing A Folder For Storing Files 31
    2.4 Configuring A Windows PC For Programming.............. 32
    2.5 Editing.. 33
    2.6 Compiling And Running.................................... 36
    2.7 Exercises, Sample Code, Videos, And Addendums............... 39

Chapter 3. Values, Variables, And Calculations 40
    3.1 Values.. 40
    3.2 Variables.. 41
    3.3 Calculations 47
    3.4 Output... 52
    3.5 Exercises, Sample Code, Videos, And Addendums............... 56

Chapter 4. Doing The Math: Libraries................ 57
    4.1 Whole Number Division And Truncation 59
    4.2 Formatting Output... 60
    4.3 More Handy Libraries And Functions................. 63
    4.4 Exercises, Sample Code, Videos, And Addendums............... 64

Chapter 5. Interactive Programs: Console I/O **65**
5.1 Capturing Values From The Keyboard 65
5.2 Prompts 68
5.3 Interrupting An Interactive Program 69
5.4 Exercises, Sample Code, Videos, And Addendums 70

PART 2: Programming Logic **71**

Chapter 6. Simple Logic: Basic Branching/Looping **73**
6.1 The If-Statement 73
6.2 Comparison Operators 75
6.3 True/False If-Statements 79
6.4 Curly-Brace Containers 80
6.5 The While-True Loop 81
6.6 The While-True-If-Break Loop 83
6.7 Bringing It All Together: Programming With Logic 85
6.8 Classic Computer Science Solutions That Use Logic 91
6.9 Exercises, Sample Code, Videos, And Addendums 93

**Chapter 7. More Than One Way: Advanced Branching/
Looping** **94**
7.1 Multiple Choice If-Statements 94
7.2 Event-Controlled vs Count-Controlled Loops 98
7.3 Introducing The For-Loop 102
7.4 Nested Loops 107
7.5 Four Forms Of The If-Statement 113
7.6 Four Forms Of Loops 115
7.7 Advanced Logic Considerations 117
7.8 Exercises, Sample Code, Videos, And Addendums 121

**Chapter 8. Simplifying Complicated Programs: Using
Functions** **122**
8.1 Value-Returning Functions 123
8.2 Parameter Lists 126
8.3 Void Functions 128
8.4 Some Examples With Functions 131
8.5 Classic Computer Science Solutions 134
8.6 Exercises, Sample Code, Videos, And Addendums 135

Chapter 9. Counting On Your Fingers: Bits And Bytes..136
9.1 Computer Memory: Vast Arrays Of On/Off Switches........136
9.2 Floating Point Numbers..140
9.3 Representing Characters 142
9.4 The True/False, Yes/No, On/Off, Up/Down, Left/
Right Data Type 143
9.5 Literal Values 144
9.6 Type Casting...145
9.7 Exercises, Sample Code, Videos, And Addendums............146

Chapter 10. Interactive Programs: File I/O....................147
10.1 Text File Input 147
10.2 Text File Output 153
10.3 Exercises, Sample Code, Videos, And Addendums..........159

PART 3: Processing Data.................................... 161

Chapter 11. Checking It Twice: Arrays 163
11.1 Array Variables...165
11.2 Array Processing...169
11.3 Dynamically-Sized Arrays 174
11.4 Arrays In Function Parameter Lists............................177
11.5 Arrays And Functions Together 178
11.6 Exercises, Sample Code, Videos, And Addendums..........182

Chapter 12. Using Objects...183
12.1 Object Specifications...183
12.2 Objects..185
12.3 Arrays Of Objects...187
12.4 Objects And Functions..188
12.5 Object-Oriented Programming 189
12.6 Exercises, Sample Code, Videos, And Addendums..........190

Chapter 13. Keeping A List: Array-Based Lists...............191
13.1 Array-Based Lists..191
13.2 Other Ways To Make Lists 200
13.3 An Array-Based List Example 200
13.4 Exercises, Sample Code, Videos, And Addendums..........203

Chapter 14. Lists Of Unlimited Size: Linked Lists **204**
14.1 The Next-Link 204
14.2 The Start-Link 205
14.3 Building A Linked List...205
14.4 Traversing Linked Lists 208
14.5 A Linked List Example 209
14.6 Linked Lists Of Whole Numbers 211
14.7 Exercises, Sample Code, Videos, And Addendums...........212

Chapter 15. Some Advanced Topics....................................**213**
15.1 The Easy Way: Collections 213
15.2 Functions That Call Themselves: Recursion.......................216
15.3 Where Do We Go From Here? 219

Appendix: The Java Library **221**

Index **223**

PART 1: The Basics

Chapter 1. Programming Concepts
1.1 The First Step, Understanding
1.2 Editors
1.3 Compilers
1.4 Elements Of Computer Languages
1.5 Exercises, Sample Code, Videos, And Addendums

Chapter 2. Editing And Compiling
2.1 Choosing An Editor
2.2 Choosing A Compiler
2.3 Choosing A Folder For Storing Files
2.4 Configuring A Windows PC For Programming
2.5 Editing
2.6 Compiling And Running
2.7 Exercises, Sample Code, Videos, And Addendums

Chapter 3. Values, Variables, And Calculations
3.1 Values
3.2 Variables
3.3 Calculations
3.4 Output
3.5 Exercises, Sample Code, Videos, And Addendums

Chapter 4. Doing The Math: Libraries
4.1 Whole Number Division And Truncation
4.2 Formatting Output
4.3 More Handy Libraries And Functions
4.4 Exercises, Sample Code, Videos, And Addendums

Chapter 5. Interactive Programs: Console I/O
5.1 Capturing Values From The Keyboard
5.2 Prompts
5.3 Interrupting An Interactive Program
5.4 Exercises, Sample Code, Videos, And Addendums

Chapter 1. Programming Concepts

Programmers give instructions to computers in the form of "computer programs". Internet Explorer, Firefox, Word, Angry Birds, TurboTax, AutoCAD, etc., are all computer programs. They were developed by programmers and are used by other people to convert their typed, touched, spoken, clicked, and pasted input into some useful or entertaining form of output. The activity whereby programmers actually create computer programs is called "programming".

Programming involves three main steps: (1) understanding the problem to be solved, (2) writing computer "code" in a human-friendly computer language, and (3) translating the code into computer-readable form (like the 0's and 1's you see in science fiction movies). The *first step* is where human intelligence comes in – you certainly must understand something before you can explain it to someone else, like a computer. The *second step* involves using another computer program known as an "editor" to write in a computer language, like Basic, C, C++, C#, Java, PHP, Python, etc. The *last step* involves using *another* computer program known as a "compiler". In this book you will learn these three steps.

1.1 The First Step, Understanding

Alas, this is the part that new programming students tend to minimize and overlook. As a result, they end up being able to create very simple programs after a couple of months of study, but are unable to progress beyond that skill level. This happens because the first examples of programming and the first assignments are usually very easy problems (like "add two and two"), and to spend any time thinking how to solve such problems seems ludicrous. It's just easier to learn the mechanics of code editing and compiling without having to also devise solutions to complicated problems. So we tend to skip directly to the second step, code editing.

This works for a while, but eventually the problems get a bit harder (like "count the number of test scores that are above the average").

That's when we get stuck, because we never developed the habit of thinking, understanding, and planning *before* coding begins.

So here's a compromise: we will not focus on understanding at first, so as not to dismiss the concept due to its apparent irrelevance. But later on in this book, when the solutions to problems are no longer obvious, the discipline of understanding and planning will be reintroduced in the form of "algorithms".

1.2 Editors

An "editor" is a program used by programmers to write computer code. Code is a set of instructions that tells the computer how to collect input, process it, and express the results as output. These instructions are not exactly written in English, although they do resemble instruction sets that you may have seen in cooking (also known as "recipes") or after you buy something that has "some assembly required".

Code is written in a "computer language". Computer languages are *simplified* and *strict* versions of English. They are simplified in the sense that they include a *very small* subset of words from the English language, such as "if", "while", "for", "break", "continue", and only a hundred or so others. Computer languages are also strict in the sense that you have to say things and punctuate things *just right*, or the computer will not understand you. You even have to spell precisely, and use uppercase where you are supposed to, and use lowercase where you are supposed to, or the computer will not know what you are talking about! It takes *intelligence* to understand nuances of language, like accents, mispronunciations, incorrect choice of words, and misspellings – and remember that it's the *humans* who have the intelligence here, and not the computers.

There are three categories of editors that are typically used for programming, as explained below: general-purpose text editors, code editors, and IDE editors.

1.2.1 Text Editors
Using the vocabulary and grammar of a computer language, programmers type instructions in an editor. Any text editor will do, including Windows **Notepad**, UNIX or Linux **vi**, and Apple MacOSx **TextEdit**. These are *general-purpose text editors*, not specifically designed for use in coding, but they work fine.

Word, Pages, and other editors capable of "rich text formatting" are not very suitable for coding. They are page-oriented, and they embed formatting information into the files they produce. While it is possible to configure such editors for text editing, it is better to avoid them.

1.2.2 Code Editors
Code editors are special-purpose text editors created specifically for code editing. Code editors may include such useful features as code templates, line numbers, and syntax highlighting. Many code editors are available on the Internet for free download and installation, or for a reasonable price. Popular ones include **Notepad++, Bluefish, TextWrangler, Emacs, Crimson, jEdit, JNotePad**, to name a few.

1.2.3 IDEs
Finally there are the editors that are bundled with high-powered, interactive development environments, or "IDEs" for short. Expensive, extensive products such as Xinox JCreator, sold to Java programmers, and Microsoft Visual Studio, sold to C++ and C# programmers, and there are many competing products. There are also free IDEs, such as Code::Blocks and Eclipse, and online IDEs, like compileonline.com. IDEs have some very useful features to help programmers, such as visual drag-and-drop development interfaces, and one-button compile-and-run.

IDEs are the most complicated of the editor choices, and beginners really should avoid them. It's possible for an introductory computer course using an IDE to be too much about the tool at the expense of the subject: programming concepts. So while any editor choice is acceptable for use as you follow this book, the examples shown here use the Windows PC **NotePad** text editor and Apple Mac **TextEdit**.

1.3 Compilers

A "compiler" is used by programmers to convert human-programmer-readable code into computer programs. Code is saved to disk files, just as any other typed document. The name of the file (ending in **.java**) identifies the file as one containing (Java language) computer code. Programs are also created as disk files. So a compiler is a computer program that takes as its input a text file, and produces as its output another file called a "program file" or "executable", typically ending in **.class** or **.jar** for Java programs.

And, yes – a programmer wrote the compiler program, which raises the chicken-and-the-egg question, but we won't get into that here.

Each compiler is designed specifically to work with a certain computer language. Hence there are Java compilers and C++ compilers, as well as compilers for every other language. So in order for you to compile, you will need to find and install a compiler program. Instructions for doing this are included elsewhere in this book.

1.4 Elements Of Computer Languages

Before you can type anything useful into an editor and save it to a file to be compiled, you need to know some basics about computer languages. There are programming concepts that are common to all computer languages, and it would be nice to write an introductory book like this at the conceptual level instead of focusing on a specific language. But it is impractical to do so. We cannot get very far without typing some code, and that means choosing a language in which to work. Java is the language used in this book.

1.4.1 Statements And Expressions
A good way to explain the basic elements of computer languages is to compare them to the written English language. Text written in the English language consists of *sentences*; computer code consists

of *statements*. While English sentences contain *phrases*, computer statements contain *expressions*.

In English	In Java
sentence: He is 21 years old.	*statement:* `int age = 21;`
phrase: over 30	*expression:* `age > 30`

In English, sentences are "read". In computer code, statements are "executed". Multiple English sentences follow one another vertically down a page. They are read in that order, and the development of thoughts depends on that order being followed. Similarly in computer code, multiple statements follow one another vertically down, and the processing of instructions depends on that order being followed. Long English sentences wrap to the next line down, and if there is still space on a line at the end of a sentence, the next sentence starts there. But wrapping is not generally used in code statements. And there is no concept of a "page". So statements in code are more like bullet points in English.

Calculating Area	
In English	**In Java**

• Measure the length.
• Measure the width.
• Multiply length and width, save as area.
• Tell me the area.
	`int length = new Double(cin.readLine()).intValue();`
	
	`int width = new Double(cin.readLine()).intValue();`
	
	`int area = length * width;`
	
	`System.out.println("The area is " + area);`

1.4.2 Sequential Processing

What's most important to understand at this point is the order in which statements are carried out. Think about giving someone driving directions – if they get the left- and right-turns out of order, they will probably end up lost! So in the above example, the statement that calculates area *must* come *after* the statements that collect values for length and width. Statements generally are not "learning experiences" for the computer. `area = length * width` is *not* telling the computer how to calculate the area of something. Instead it is an instruction that says to take the values currently stored as **length** and as **width**, multiply them, and save the result as **area**.

Below are examples of sequential processing presented as "recipes", in which numbered steps are processed from the top, down. Of course, we don't use the word "recipe" in computer programs – we call them "algorithms" instead:

Macaroni and Cheese	Area Of A Room
1 Preheat oven broiler.	1 Write labels "length" and "width" on paper.
2 Bring a large pot of water to a boil.	2 Measure length of room, in decimal feet.
3 Add pasta to pot and cook 9 minutes.	3 Write length on paper next to its label.
4 Drain the pot.	4 Measure width of room, in decimal feet.
5 Add pasta to a 2 qt dish.	5 Write width on paper next to its label.
6 Shred cheese and add to dish.	6 Using a calculator, enter the length.
7 Add milk to dish.	7 On the calculator, press **x**.
8 Stir pasta, cheese, and milk in dish.	8 On the calculator, enter the width.
9 Microwave dish for 2 minutes.	9 On the calculator, press **=**.
10 Broil dish for 3 minutes.	10 Write result on paper, with label "area".

This concept of sequential processing of statements is a key concept in programming.

1.4.3 Entry Point

The first statement to execute when a program starts is the "entry point" for the program. This seems like an obvious concept and not worthy of mention – isn't the first statement the one that appears on the first line of the code's file? Actually, it's not that easy. Come to think of it, it's not so easy in English either. In books, doesn't the first line of the first chapter usually come after the title page, the copyright page, and the preface and prologue? It's the same with coding. There are titles and prologues that come before the first statement. So when we get to actual code examples later, we will have to be aware that there will be prologue material, and there will have to be a way to identify the "entry point".

The next example adds some preparatory information at the top of the previous sequential processing example, to illustrate the concept of "entry point":

Macaroni and Cheese

INGREDIENTS
1 cup elbow macaroni pasta
1/4 cup milk
1-1/2 cups cheddar cheese

DIRECTIONS
entry point 1 Preheat oven broiler.
2 Bring a large pot of water to a boil.
3 Add pasta to pot and cook 9 minutes.
4 Drain the pot.
5 Add pasta to a 2 qt dish.
6 Shred cheese and add to dish.
7 Add milk to dish.
8 Stir pasta, cheese, and milk in dish.
9 Microwave dish for 2 minutes.
10 Broil dish for 3 minutes.

1.4.4 Branching And Looping

But starting at an entry point and executing every statement in sequential order does not provide enough flexibility for most purposes. What if the "width" is not entered correctly in the above example? What if the person using the program types "ten" instead of "10"? What if they enter a negative number, or a number that is way higher than is reasonable? There should be a way to skip the calculation and provide the user with some... constructive feedback. Or what if the user has more than one area calculation to make? Should they have to restart the program again and again? Wouldn't it be better if the program started itself over automatically?

To accommodate these needs, computer programming includes the concepts of *branching* and *looping*. Branching enables one set of statements to be executed under some conditions, and another set under other conditions. This programming feature is illustrated with instructions to skip down (or *branch*) to a later statement. Looping enables a program to repeat itself. This programming feature is illustrated with instructions to skip up (or *loop back*) to a previous statement.

Here are some algorithm samples in which numbered steps are processed from the top, down:

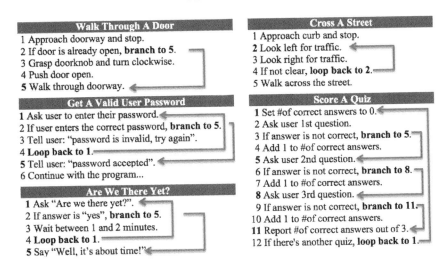

Walk Through A Door
1 Approach doorway and stop.
2 If door is already open, **branch to 5**.
3 Grasp doorknob and turn clockwise.
4 Push door open.
5 Walk through doorway.

Cross A Street
1 Approach curb and stop.
2 Look left for traffic.
3 Look right for traffic.
4 If not clear, **loop back to 2**.
5 Walk across the street.

Get A Valid User Password
1 Ask user to enter their password.
2 If user enters the correct password, **branch to 5**.
3 Tell user: "password is invalid, try again".
4 **Loop back to 1**.
5 Tell user: "password accepted".
6 Continue with the program...

Score A Quiz
1 Set #of correct answers to 0.
2 Ask user 1st question.
3 If answer is not correct, **branch to 5**.
4 Add 1 to #of correct answers.
5 Ask user 2nd question.
6 If answer is not correct, **branch to 8**.
7 Add 1 to #of correct answers.
8 Ask user 3rd question.
9 If answer is not correct, **branch to 11**.
10 Add 1 to #of correct answers.
11 Report #of correct answers out of 3.
12 If there's another quiz, **loop back to 1**.

Are We There Yet?
1 Ask "Are we there yet?".
2 If answer is "yes", **branch to 5**.
3 Wait between 1 and 2 minutes.
4 **Loop back to 1**.
5 Say "Well, it's about time!"

Study the examples provided above, and see if you can identify where *branching* is used, and where *looping* is used. After we gain enough skill to use sequential processing effectively in our programs, we will introduce the concepts of branching and looping. Look for this in the first chapter of Part 2.

1.4.5 Subprograms

For very complex programs it is convenient for the programmer to break down a large problem into several smaller problems – kind of a divide-and-conquer approach. Computer languages support the concept of subprograms. We do the same in the English language, when we provide details in web page links or in book appendices or Post-it notes.

For example, we will learn to write programs that ask the user for input. Our programs will "validate" the input (that is, make sure it is valid) before continuing with their processing. For invalid input, these programs will alert the user and offer another chance to enter valid input. As you can imagine, this involves a lot of detail – certainly some branching and looping will be included somewhere.

Here is an example that uses a subprogram to manage the details of the area calculation, using "jumps" between the main flow of the program and the subprogram, with lines and arrows showing the flow of the program:

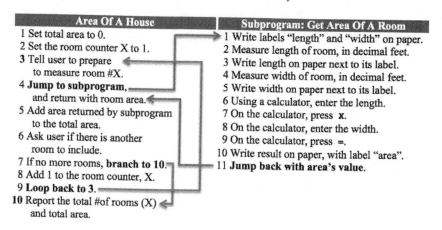

Area Of A House	Subprogram: Get Area Of A Room
1 Set total area to 0.	1 Write labels "length" and "width" on paper.
2 Set the room counter X to 1.	2 Measure length of room, in decimal feet.
3 Tell user to prepare to measure room #X.	3 Write length on paper next to its label.
4 **Jump to subprogram**, and return with room area.	4 Measure width of room, in decimal feet.
5 Add area returned by subprogram to the total area.	5 Write width on paper next to its label.
6 Ask user if there is another room to include.	6 Using a calculator, enter the length.
7 If no more rooms, **branch to 10.**	7 On the calculator, press **x**.
8 Add 1 to the room counter, X.	8 On the calculator, enter the width.
9 **Loop back to 3.**	9 On the calculator, press =.
10 Report the total # of rooms (X) and total area.	10 Write result on paper, with label "area".
	11 **Jump back with area's value.**

The code for large programs can be obscured by the endless details of such simple operations. So detail is typically removed to subprograms (usually called "methods" in Java, but what we'll call "functions" in this book), and represented by a single statement directing the processing temporarily to the subprogram for the details of the operation. Look for this in the middle chapters of Part 2.

1.5 Exercises, Sample Code, Videos, And Addendums

Go to www.rdb3.com/java/1 for exercises that are suitable for lab assignments. They can be used exactly as they are, or copied, pasted, and marked up by instructors for use in their classes.

There are also some samples of solutions to other exercises to show students the format and detail they should expect to apply in solving the exercises. And there's a YouTube-like video, explaining the concepts presented in this chapter.

You'll find a similar URL at the end of each chapter of this book with extended information on the chapter's topic. New material gets added from time to time, especially in chapters where the details are affected by advances in technology, like chapter 2, which is about operating systems and compiler software – technologies that change constantly.

Also, contributors are encouraged to send new materials to the author for possible inclusion in the chapter's extended information.

Chapter 2. Editing And Compiling

Now that the main concepts of programming have been explained, it's time to actually do some programming. In order for you to "edit" and "compile" a program, you'll need a program to type, an editor, and a compiler program. At first, what you will type will be provided for you – you'll type exactly what this book tells you to type. But as we move forward, you'll have more and more of an opportunity to write parts yourself, and ultimately write whole programs yourself.

Some of the instructions for editing and compiling are "system-dependent" – that is, they depend on whether you are using a Windows PC or a Mac or something else. The presentation in this chapter is specific to Microsoft Windows on a PC and Apple OSX on a Mac. But where it's appropriate to do so, alternate instructions for UNIX/Linux are included.

Here's a checklist of the things you will need to consider:

Checklist
✓ Choose an editor. Install, if necessary. Configure for your use.
✓ Choose a compiler. Install, if necessary. Configure for your use.
✓ Choose a folder on your system for storing your files.
✓ Configure your PC (if you are using Microsoft Windows)

Once this checklist is completed, you will be ready to edit and compile your first program in Java!

2.1 Choosing An Editor

The first thing to do is to choose an editor. Our choice for PCs is **Notepad**, which can be found under Start|All Programs|Accessories|Notepad. No installation is necessary for **Notepad**. Our choice for Mac is **TextEdit**, which can be found in Finder under Applications – also no installation.

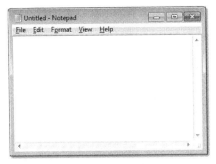
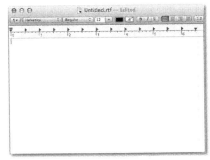

Notepad on a PC   TextEdit on a Mac

2.1.1 Configuring Notepad On A Windows PC

Two settings need to be made in **Notepad**, so that you can see "line numbers". The first is to turn off "word wrap" – to do so, use the Format menu. Make sure that there is no checkmark next to the "Word Wrap" option. If there is, click it to make it go away. Then turn on the "status bar". To do so, use the View menu. If there is a checkmark beside "Status Bar", leave it. Otherwise, click it. The Format and View menus should look like this when you're done:

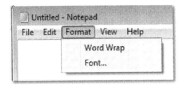

On your own computer these settings will persist from session to session. But in the computer lab, you probably will have to configure these each time you sit at a computer workstation.

2.1.2 Configuring TextEdit On A Mac

For Mac TextEdit, the default configuration is for "rich text". That will *not* do for programming. So go to the Format menu and click "Make Plain Text". Thereafter the menu will show "Make Rich Text" instead, and the edit window will look like the one on the right.

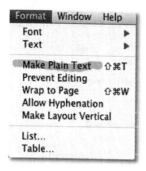
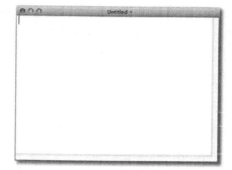

2.1.3 Installing JNotePad

The **JNotePad** editor was written by the author of this book. It is similar to **Notepad** and **TextEdit**, except that it works on almost any operating system, including Windows, OSX, and versions of Linux with a graphical user interface. It also contains menu-accessible Java (and C++) "code block" templates that match the examples in this book. Also, JNotePad is a good choice if you plan to go back and forth between a PC and a Mac, because it automatically deals with the extra blank lines and the loss of line breaks that happen with files that get traded back and forth between Macs and PCs. The JNotePad window looks like the one shown here.

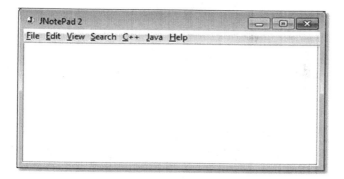

The installation of **JNotePad** is *very* easy – it just involves copying its startup icon from the Internet URL www.rdb3.com/jnotepad to your desktop or flash drive. Users of Mac computers can start using JNotePad right away for Java program editing. But in order for Windows PC users to use the icon, they first need to download and install either the "Java SE *JRE*" or the "Java SE *JDK*" from the

Internet URL www.oracle.com/technetwork/java/javase/downloads, where the latest version at the time of this writing is Java SE 8u25. For Java compiling, you need the JDK, as explained below. The lighter JRE is just for *running* programs that others (like yourself and like the author of JNotePad) wrote in Java.

2.2 Choosing A Compiler

Selection of a compiler depends on the chosen language and the system being used. Compiler options for Java on Windows PCs, Macs, Linux, and UNIX are presented below.

The Java compiler works the same on all systems. Your system may already have a Java compiler installed on it. To find out, go to a "command prompt" (using Start|All Programs|Accessories|Command Prompt on a PC, or the Terminal app in the Mac's Applications folder), and enter the command `javac -version`. If a version number appears (like "javac 1.7.0_51"), then you have a Java compiler. Any version 1.6 or higher will be suitable for following the examples in this book, and doing the exercises at the end of each chapter.

But if you have an earlier version, or if your PC says "not recognized" or "bad command", or your Mac says "No Java runtime present, requesting install", then you'll need to install Java. To do so, use the following installation instructions for PCs and/or Mac. Otherwise, all is on order, and you can skip down to section 2.2.3.

2.2.1 Installing The Java Compiler On A Windows PC
Download and install from the Java download page, www.oracle.com/technetwork/java/javase/downloads, where the latest version at the time of this writing is Java SE 8u25.

The compiler download is about 70 MB in size. To find it on the Oracle website, use the "Java SE" download link, and then follow the link to download the latest "Java SE Development Kit" JDK (*not the JRE*). Then download and install the version of the Development Kit that matches your system (Windows, etc.), following all defaults. You can delete the approximately 70MB installation file after you are finished with the installation. Note that the commands mentioned above may not work, even after this installation. That is because you still need to configure the compiler, as explained in section 2.2.4 below.

2.2.2 Installing The Java Compiler On A Mac

On a Mac, you can get to the Java download page, www.oracle.com/technetwork/java/javase/downloads, by clicking the "More Info..." button on the popup that appears after unsuccessfully running the **javac -version** command, like this:

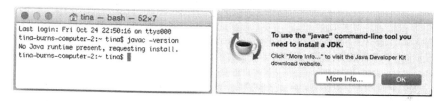

Follow the prompts to install the latest JDK – *not the JRE!*

2.2.3 Using An Online Compiler

Alternatively you can use a fully online compiler like the one at ideone.com. Copy/paste your own code into its online edit box, but just remember to replace the word "public class" with just "class" before running it online. You'll learn about "public class" in section 2.5 below. And remember to specify that the language is Java in the list of languages that the website supports. Don't rely on ideone.com for your programming assignments, but it does offer handy access to a compiler when you need one.

2.2.4 Configuring Your Java Compiler On A Windows PC

Once a compiler is installed on a PC, it is important to confirm that it is in fact working correctly. Even if your compiler of choice was pre-installed, it is still important to perform the same confirmation steps as if you yourself installed it.

After the Java SE Development Kit is installed, you need to type some configuration commands. First locate the file **javac.exe**, which should be in the **bin** folder of your Java compiler installation.

This folder should be **C:\Program Files\Java\jdk1.7.0_02\bin**, or something similar, for a default installation of JDK.

Note that there may be a different name for the **jdk1.7.0_02** folder on your Windows system. You may even have more than one installation, each with its own **bin** folder and **javac.exe**. If so, pick the latest one. Once you determine the JDK folder name for your system, modify the following instructions to use that folder name instead of **jdk1.7.0_02**.

Every time you begin a session of Java compiling, you will need to get a command prompt (as explained above), and enter 2 commands. The first is `path=C:\Program Files\ Java\jdk1.7.0_02\bin;%path%`. The second is `set classpath=`.

There is no feedback or other output produced by either of these commands, but the `javac -version` command should work now. (On your own computer, you may want to create a file named **java.se.bat** containing these two commands. Store it in your **c:\ windows** folder, and you only have to type the command `java.se` instead.)

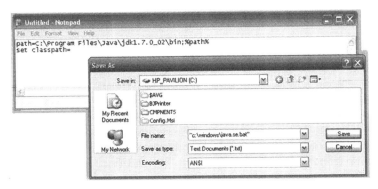

30

2.3 Choosing A Folder For Storing Files

To store your Java "source files" on a PC or Mac and do your programming work, you should have a folder reserved specifically for that purpose. This is called your "working folder". Decide upon this and get it ready *before* writing your first program.

You can put your working folder on a hard drive or on removable media, like a flash drive. If you are not yet comfortable with "command line" mode or file structure navigation, it's easiest to simply use a flash drive or a cloud folder. Also, with your files on a flash drive they are readily portable between home and classroom and lab, and so on – even between PC and Mac. The rest of this section is organized for students using flash drives, as others with more experience can easily adapt the instructions for themselves.

On a PC, use Windows Explorer to create your working folder on your flash drive. On a Mac, your flash drive icon should already appear on your desktop with a default name, like "NO NAME". You can rename it as you would rename any file or folder on your Mac desktop. It's better to name it *without spaces* – something like `programming`, and thereafter it will appear on your desktop like this:

Now create your working folder on your flash drive, named for example, `java`. While it's possible to put this folder inside some other folder on the flash drive, the rest of this section is written as though the working folder is *not* inside some other folder.

Next, figure out how to locate your working folder in command line mode. On a PC, open a command prompt window as explained previously. Navigate to your flash drive by typing the letter designation of the drive, then a colon, and then press ENTER. That is, enter the command `e:` if your flash drive designation is "E".

Then navigate to your working folder using a command like `cd\java`, for example.

On a Mac, start the Terminal app and enter the command `cd /volumes/programming/java`, for example. That's `cd`, not `CD`, and it's slash `/`, not backslash `\`. And don't forget the space after `cd` on the Mac.

Or on either Mac or PC, type `cd` , drag and drop your working folder onto it, and press ENTER. That's C D *space*, not just C D. Then you can do the drag and drop to complete the command, and then press ENTER.

2.3.1 How To Backup Your Files

The rule is simple: "only backup the files that you do not want to lose." After you finish editing your source files, and save them onto a hard drive or flash drive, imagine for a moment what would happen if the hard drive fails tonight or you misplace your flash drive. It's a good idea to backup your files by putting a copy of them on the Internet. There are several free options, including emailing attachments to yourself, and file hosting services like Dropbox and Google Drive. If you are doing assignments for a computer course you are taking, the course may even offer a class website for submitting your files, and you could use that to backup your work.

Decide on your own process for backing up your work, and make it a habit to email or upload your files at the end of each work session.

2.4 Configuring A Windows PC For Programming

Actually, you can use PCs for programming without any configuration changes. But there is one change that makes things easier for identifying files, and it is *highly* recommended. The problem is that Windows hides filename extensions by default. That is, the compiled program's file **Hello.class** may appear only partially – that is, without the dot and the "class" after the dot – in a file listing. To change this behavior, start **Windows Explorer** from its icon, which looks like this in Windows 8:

Then use the menu command "Organize|Folder and Search Options". Click the "View" tab, and remove the checkmark from "Hide extensions for known file types".

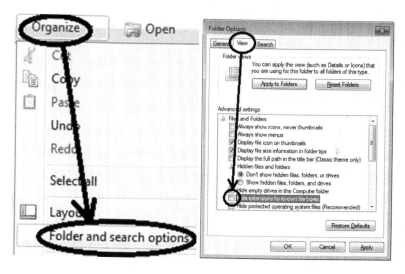

The Windows 7 folder options are also located in the Control Panel, under Appearance and Personalization. Look for Folder Options, then the View tab, and then uncheck "Hide extensions for known file types". Click OK and then close.

On your own computer, this setting will persist from session to session. But in a computer lab, you may have to configure this each time. Note that Macs do not hide filename extensions, so no configuration is necessary.

2.5 Editing

Okay – we are ready to program! Let's start by writing the world's smallest Java program, and compiling and running that. It actually doesn't do anything, but if you are able to get this far, then you can at least establish that you can use an editor and that you have a compiler. With these details out of the way, we can focus on learning to program! Here's our first program:

```
World's Smallest Java Program
public class Hello
{
  public static void main(String[] argv)
  {
  }
}
```

Start up your text editor. The examples in this book are shown in Windows **Notepad**, but you can use any other editor and system. So if you are using a Mac, you can use **TextEdit**, configured for plain text. And if you are using Linux or UNIX, use **vi** or any other text editor with which you are familiar.

Note that there are some lines containing "curly-braces". Also notice that some lines are indented from the left margin, and others start at the left margin. Use *2 spaces* to indent. It is possible to use a tab instead of 2 spaces, and many programmers do just that. But tab sizes are variable among editors, so that if you look at your code in one editor, it may not look the same as it does in another editor. Worse, if you use spaces sometimes and tabs sometimes, what looks fine in one editor may look misaligned in another.

2.5.1 How To Type Code

The tendency is to type code "linearly" – that is, from the top line to the bottom. But that is not the best way to type code. Matching parentheses and curly-braces appear throughout code. The toughest part is to keep track of these and make sure that each open parenthesis has a matching closing parenthesis. The easiest way to do that is to type opening and closing symbols together, and then separate them.

In the "World's Smallest Java Program" above, and any other program you write, you should type an opening parenthesis followed immediately by its matching closing parenthesis. Then put your edit cursor between the two and type its contents -- **"String[] argv"** in the example above. The two pairs of curly-brace symbols { and } form two "curly-brace containers", one inside the other. Always type a set of curly-braces *together*, typing the closing } *immediately below and aligned with* the opening {. Then put your edit cursor after the opening { and press ENTER a few times to make space to put code inside the container. In the case above, create the *outer* container first, then the *inner*.

Note that as you type the program, there is an indication on the editor about the line number that is currently being edited. In **Notepad** this is located in the lower right with the abbreviations "Ln" for line number and "Col" for column number. (If this does not appear, then revisit section 2.1.1 above.) This is not so important for now, but knowing the line number will be important when we get to the compiling step, in case the compiler detects and reports typing errors. Unfortunately the line number does not appear in TextEdit on a Mac – one reason why JNotePad may be the better choice for an editor.

2.5.2 Saving A File

Save the file as **Hello.java**, into the "working folder" you created for storing your programming files (**e:\rdb** on a PC in the examples in this book). If you use **Notepad** on a PC, you may have to enclose the filename in quotes, or else **.txt** may be appended to the filename! The saved file is called the "source file", and it contains "source code". It should look something like this on PCs and Macs:

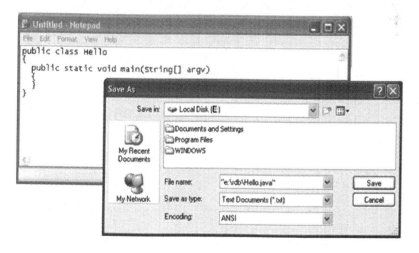

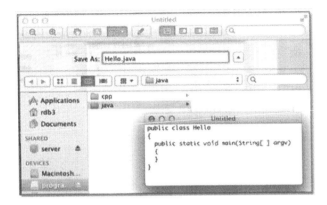

2.6 Compiling And Running

Now that the program's source file has been saved to the drive, you are ready to compile it into a working program file!

First, go to a command prompt as explained above, and navigate to the drive and working folder containing your edited source file. It should look like this on a PC or Mac, with what *you* would type appearing like this: `cd\rdb` in the PC screen shots, and like this: `cd /Volumes/programming/rdb` in the Mac screenshots:

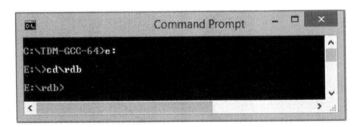

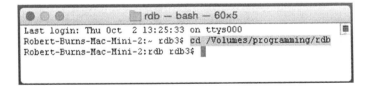

2.6.1 How To Compile

Here's how to **COMPILE** it. Invoke the Java compiler by typing this command, on a PC or Mac command line:

```
javac Hello.java
```

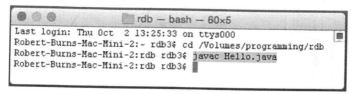

If there are any errors, it should be evident from the output of the compiler. Line numbers should also appear in the output of the compiler, guiding you to the problem. Otherwise, here's how to **RUN** it:

2.6.2 How To Run

If successful, the Java compiler will have created **Hello.class** in the same folder. This is the actual program file that the computer will run. You can distribute this file to people, and they will be able to run it – although those with Windows PCs may have to install a Java JRE or JDK first. To run, type this command on a PC or Mac:

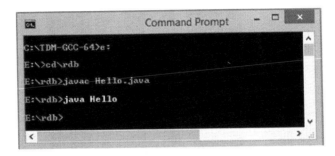

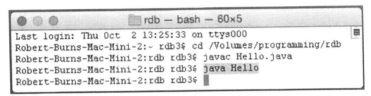

Don't be disappointed if nothing happens – remember that this is the world's smallest Java program, and it does nothing. It collects no input and it produces no output. But at least it does not produce an error!

In this very simple programming example, you completed the editing step before you started the compiling step, and completed that before running. In *all other* cases you will mix these steps – that is, you will write part of the code, save, compile, and run, and then write more code and repeat this process. Just remember to save and compile and run often.

Also, you should backup your work at the end of every editing session. Backup only the source files that you type – there is no need to backup any files generated by the compiler.

2.6.3 Recompiling

When you use the command line to compile your programs, it will seem as if there is a lot of typing to do – repetitive typing. But you do not have to retype the compile command over and over again. PCs and Macs both let you use the UP and DOWN ARROWs of the keyboard to recall a recently typed command. On PCs, you can also use the F7 key to get a menu of recently typed commands, although the UP ARROW is the easiest way to recall the last-typed command.

2.7 Exercises, Sample Code, Videos, And Addendums

Go to www.rdb3.com/java/2 for extended materials pertaining to this chapter.

Chapter 3. Values, Variables, And Calculations

Make sure that you have figured out the steps for editing and saving source files and that you can compile and run your programs before proceeding with this chapter. You may change your choice of compilers or systems during your study, and that's okay. It's good for a computer programmer to work independent of any specific system, editor, or compiler. But for now, find something that works for you and try to stick with it as you go through the first part of this book.

Now that you have figured out how to create computer programs in Java, let's do something a bit more interesting. This section introduces the concepts of data "values", "variables" for storing data values, and "calculations" for processing data. It covers the three parts of simple programs: assigning input values, performing calculations using those values, and displaying output. The techniques explained in this chapter will enable you to write programs that can do calculations like Excel spreadsheets can do.

3.1 Values

A "value" is a piece of information used in a computer program. Values can be combined in such simple operations as addition, or processed in more complicated operations like spell checking. Values can be specified by the programmer, entered by a user, or read from a disk file – all of which are covered in this book. There are two distinct types of values used in computer programs: *numbers* and *text* (or words).

The ways in which computers remember, process, and display data values depends on whether the values are numeric or text. It's as if computers had "left brain/right brain" separation, which is the concept that we humans process logic with the left side of our brains and emotion with the right side. Similarly, computers have one way of "thinking about" numbers, and another way for text. So in computer programming, for each step that involves data values of some kind, the computer has to be "told" that "we're working with numbers now", or "get ready to handle some text".

Actually, it gets a bit more specific in Java programming, because not only is there a distinction between numbers and text, there are finer distinctions within those categories. Numbers can be either whole numbers, as might be used in counting (like 1, 2, 3, etc.), or they can allow fraction or decimal parts, as might be used to record grade point average (for example, 3.24) or temperature (like 98.6 degrees F). Similarly, text can be either single letters (or "characters"), as might be used to record a grade (like A, B, C, etc.), or they can be multiple characters, as might be used to represent someone's name.

You might wonder why we would even bother with this. Can't the fractional or decimal part of a value be zero? And can't a word consist of a single letter? So why have special categories for whole numbers and single characters? The reason is that there are certain efficiencies in the ways that computers deal with the simpler forms of numbers and text. The simplest numbers are whole numbers, and the simplest words consist of 1 letter. So in dealing with numeric values, if we can use elements of the computer language that are intended for whole numbers, we do so. Otherwise we use the more general ways of dealing with numbers that may or may not have fractional parts. Likewise in dealing with text values, if we can use elements of the computer language that are intended for single characters, we do so. Otherwise we use the more general ways of dealing with text that may have any number of characters, even zero (as would be used to represent a blank).

3.2 Variables

A "variable" is something in a computer program that programmers use to store a value. People can remember values by writing them on paper – computers use "variables". Sometimes data values are specified in a program's code, written there by the *programmer*. Other times the source of the data value is input, as from a keyboard or text file (as we will study in chapters 5 and 10 of this book), allowing a *user* of the program to specify them.

Still other times the source is the result of a calculation made in the program, such as calculating area based on length and width, and using that to calculate how much paint to buy. In any case, variables are simply the things that store data values in a computer program.

3.2.1 Identifiers

Variables have names, or "identifiers". On paper, people might write labels or other descriptions by the values they write, so they remember what the values mean. Computers use "identifiers" to do the same thing. By referring to the name of a variable in a computer program, its associated data can be stored or retrieved. The memory used by variables is typically recyclable – that is, you can store a new value in a variable (after you are finished with the old value, of course). Similarly, people can cross out or erase previously written values and write new ones, like keeping score of a ball game.

Variable names are chosen by the programmer, who can select just about anything. But there are some *rules*: the name must consist of one or more lowercase letters, uppercase letters, digits, and/ or underscore symbols – no spaces are allowed! Also, the name may not begin with a digit, and it cannot be the same as one of the hundred or so words used in the language (called "keywords"), such as "if" and "while". For example, `age` could be used for a variable that stores a person's age.

Besides the rules, there are some *conventions* which most programmers follow: variables usually begin with a lowercase letter. Also, identifiers consisting of more than one word, since they cannot be separated by spaces, are run together with the first character in each word after the first being uppercase. For example, `firstName` could be used for a variable that stores a person's first name.

The number of variables that a programmer can use in a program is basically limited by the amount of memory in the computer. For today's desktop computers, notebooks, tablets, and smart phones, it is *practically* unlimited.

3.2.2 Declaration Statements

So for each item of data to be stored, there needs to be a variable. To create a variable in a Java program, you have to specify two things: a unique identifier for the variable, and *the type of data to store* in the variable. This specification must be made as a *statement*, and it is called a "declaration statement". To reserve memory to store a numeric value in a variable named "age", it looks something like this:

Representation in code   Conceptual representation

Note the semicolon at the end of the statement. Statements usually end in a semicolon.

You probably expected the part about a declaration statement involving a variable name. But there is another part of the declaration statement that you should have seen coming as a result of the discussion about values – specification of the *data type*. That is, the computer needs to be told something about the kind of data that will be stored in the variable being declared, so that it can reserve memory accordingly. This is a requirement of the Java computer language – C++, too. If you programmed in Basic or Javascript before, this was *not* a requirement of those languages. So that's what the "int" is doing in the above declaration statement.

"int" is a *keyword* in Java. It means "integer", which is a whole number, positive or negative. Integers have no fractional parts to them. Negative values have a minus prepended to them, but positive numbers do *not* have plus signs – numbers are positive unless otherwise specified. Another numeric *data type* includes "double" for double-precision floating-point numbers (with possible fractional parts). There are also data types for text: "char" for single-character text and "string" for longer (or shorter!) text. "char" is pronounced like the word "care", as the first syllable in the word "character". And note that "string" is *capitalized* in Java like this: "String".

Some Data Types In Java	
int	for storing whole numbers, like 12 or 0 or -99
double	for storing floating point numbers, like 1.534 or 100.0
char	for storing 1-character text, such as 'T' or 'F' (true or false), or 'A', 'B',... (grades), or digits '0', '1',..., or punctuation symbols ';', '.',...
String	for storing Java text of any length, such as "I am learning how to program!"

Actually, most programming textbooks use the keyword "float" for single-precision floating-point numbers, instead of "double" as is used here. The reason for using "double" instead of "float" is that it is more directly compatible with "literal values", which we will learn about in chapter 9.

So to declare a variable for storing text, you could use a statement like **String firstName;**. Declarations cannot be put just anywhere in the code – they need to be placed *after* the **{** that immediately follows the line with the word "main", and *before* its matching **}** – that is, *inside* main's curly-brace container.

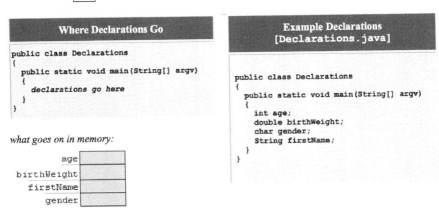

Note the indenting of the lines containing the declaration statements. Indenting is not important to the compiler – it is only for human-readability and organization of code. Note also that:

The name in the first line is "Declarations". It was "Hello" in the previous example. Because of this, the file *must be named* **Declarations.java**. In Java, the public class name *must match* the file's name.

- The data type and the identifier are separated by a single space, but it can be more than one if desired for alignment of the code.
- Each declaration statement ends with a semicolon.

As we introduce you to new types of statements in the remainder of this chapter, you should consider starting up your editor and your compiler, and experiment by typing similar code and seeing if you can compile and run it!

3.2.3 Assignment Upon Declaration

Now that we have variables, values can be stored in them via the keyboard or as a result of a calculation. There are 5 basic ways to store values in a variable: (1) by specifying a value upon declaration, (2) by assigning or reassigning a value anytime after declaration, (3) by performing a calculation and storing the result, (4) by transferring a value from the keyboard, and (5) by transferring a value from a text file. (The latter 2 of these will be studied in chapters 5 and 10 of this book).

To specify a value *upon declaration*, use a statement like `int age = 21;` . This statement does two things at once – it reserves memory for whole number named "age", and it stores the value 21 in it. Note that there are single spaces surrounding the equal sign – they are not required by the compiler, but are put there for better human readability. Here are some other examples of *assignment upon declaration*:

Examples Of Assignment Upon Declaration	
`int age = 21;`	the number is a *whole number*, with no fractional part possible
`double pi = 3.14;`	the number has a decimal point in it, to allow for a fractional part (if any)
`double temperature = 72;`	it's okay for a floating point value to have no fractional part – either append `.0` or leave it off
`char gender = 'M';`	1-character "char" values are offset by *single* quote marks, or apostrophes. They are *unformatted*: not 'or ' – it's just '.
`String name = "George Washington";`	any-length text values are offset by double *quote* marks – even if they are empty (""). They are *unformatted*: not " or " – it's just ".

age	21
pi	3.14
temperature	72
gender	M
name	George Washington

3.2.4 Assignment Statements

To change a value *after* a variable's declaration, use a statement like `age = 21;`, leaving off the data type specification. This is known as an "assignment statement", and it can only be used *after* `age` is declared. Remember *sequential processing*? It is okay to reassign values to variables as often as you like, whether or not they were initialized upon declaration. But you can declare a variable only once, because of the uniqueness requirement for identifiers (that is, variable names). Here are some other examples of *assignment statements*:

Examples Of Assignment Statements	
`age = 30;`	"age" must have already been declared in a preceding statement
`temperature = 99.7;`	this works fine if "temperature" was already declared as a "double", but if it was declared as an "int", it causes a compiler error in Java!
`grade = 'A';`	"grade" must have already been declared in a preceding statement
`name = "Pres. Washington";`	the number of characters in the text does *not* have to be the same when reassigning a new text value

In Java, you *cannot* use a variable in a calculation or in output until a value is assigned to it. If you try, an error occurs during compilation, and the output of the compiler explains that you tried to use a variable before it was "initialized".

3.3 Calculations

Once there are variables with valid values, they can be considered as inputs to calculations. Calculations take place in *expressions*, which usually involve variables, numbers, and an *operation symbol*, like a plus sign. For example, `a + b` is an expression that results in adding the values stored in 2 variables, named "a" and "b". Note that for this expression to be valid, both `a` and `b` must have been declared and assigned values *before* the expression appears.

In an expression like `a + b`, the `a` and `b` are called "operands". An operand in a calculation expression can be a variable name, as shown in the examples so far, or they can be values. For example, `10 + 17`, `a + 5`, or `7 + b`, are all valid calculation expressions, or "math operations".

Some other simple math operations besides addition are subtraction (`a − b`), multiplication (`a * b`), and division (`a / b`). There is also modulus (`a % b`) which results in the *remainder* of the whole number division problem "b goes into a... with the remainder...". You know how to use addition, subtraction, multiplication, and division. Here's how some of these work:

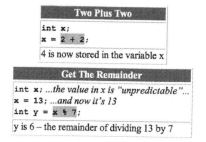

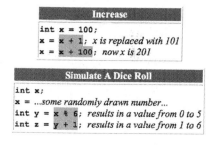

Calculation expressions can have numbers as operands as well as variables, like `a / 3` and `2 + 2`. They almost always involve two values and an operation symbol in between.

3.3.1 Using Calculation Expressions In Statements
Remember that expressions do not stand alone – they have to be used in statements. In the same way, words in English do not stand

alone – they need to be used in sentences in order to be understood in the proper context. The simplest way to use a calculation expression in a statement is to use it in an *assignment statement*. For example, `c = a + b;`. This statement performs the addition of "a" and "b", and stores the result in the variable named "c", reusing "c" by overwriting what was there before.

Note that the equal sign in the assignment statement is *not* the same as the equal sign in mathematics! In math it is used to express equivalence between the two sides of the equal sign. In programming, it means to evaluate the expression on the *right side* of the equal sign, and store the result in the variable on the *left* side of the equal sign. It does *not* establish equivalence for the computer to remember and apply where appropriate – remember: sequential processing! You cannot put anything except for a single variable on the left side.

So here are two ways to add 2 and 2, one using assignment upon declaration, and the other using separate declaration and assignment statements. Either way is fine. Note that neither one of these examples includes any kind of output to the display monitor! This will be considered at the end of chapter 3.

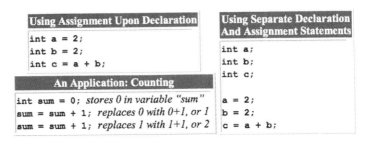

Look at the counting application above and see if you can understand what is going on there. Note that it involves *replacing* what is stored in the declared variable. Variables can remember multiple values in a program, but only one of them at a time. The statement `sum = sum + 1;` reads like this: "Retrieve what is stored in sum and add 1 to it. Then store the result in sum, replacing what was there". In assignment statements, resolve what is on the *right-hand side of the equal sign* first, and then store the resulting value in the variable that appears on the *left-hand side of the equal sign*. Never put anything other than a single variable's name to the left of the equal sign, as you see in all the above examples.

Here is another example of some simple calculations, shown as two possible ways to do the same thing. Note that a variable can only be declared *once* – that is why in the previous example you do not see a statement like `int a;` followed later by `int a = 2;`. Instead, you see `int a;` followed later by `a = 2;`, which avoids declaring the variable `a` a second time. Note that the same is true about the variables in the following example:

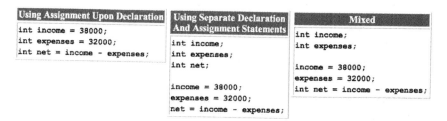

Using Assignment Upon Declaration	Using Separate Declaration And Assignment Statements	Mixed

`int income = 38000;`
`int expenses = 32000;`
`int net = income - expenses;`
	`int income;`
	`int expenses;`
	`int net;`
	
	`income = 38000;`
	`expenses = 32000;`
	`net = income - expenses;`
		`int income;`
		`int expenses;`
		
		`income = 38000;`
		`expenses = 32000;`
		`int net = income - expenses;`

In each of the above, the variables are declared once, and only once.

3.3.2 Complex Expressions

Math operations in computer languages involve 2 values. But we often have to solve problems with more than 2 values, such as the average of 3 numbers. So how is that done using programming languages? First realize that the averaging of 3 numbers is really a series of 2-value operations. Add the first and second numbers together. Then add the third number. Finally, divide by three. Calculators work this way – do an operation with 2 numbers, then use that result as the first number in the next 2-value operation, and so on. Multiple-step calculations can be done by breaking them down into steps involving only two values. So we can write this in a series of statements, or we can use complex expressions that let us combine a series of 2-value expressions into a single statement. Here are three ways to find the average of 3 numbers:

Using Simple Expressions	Using Complex Expressions

`int age1 = 19;`
`int age2 = 21;`
`int age3 = 30;`
`int averageAge;`
 	
`averageAge = age1 + age2;`
`averageAge = averageAge + age3;`
`averageAge = averageAge / 3;`
	`int age1 = 19;`
	`int age2 = 21;`
	`int age3 = 30;`
	`int averageAge = ((age1 + age2) + age3) / 3;`
	`...or...`
	`int averageAge = (age1 + age2 + age3) / 3;`

In the simple expressions solution, note the statement `averageAge = averageAge + age3;`. This is a kind of assignment statement will *overwrite* an existing value with a new value. Remember that data stored in memory can be replaced when it is no longer needed.

The parentheses (in the solution with complex expressions) enclose and isolate one 2-value operation, so that it can be completed and the result *substituted* into the remaining expression. So `((age1 + age2) + age3) / 3` resolves to `((19 + 21) + age3) / 3` resolves to `(40 + age3) / 3` resolves to `(40 + 30) / 3` resolves to `70 / 3`, etc.

Actually it is acceptable to write this as `(age1 + age2 + age3) / 3`, because computer languages treat multiple successive additions as through they were paired in parentheses. But it's *not* okay to write it as `age1 + age2 + age3 / 3`, because that mixes addition and multiplication. In such cases, the multiplications (and divisions) are done first in the order in which they appear, left to right. Then the additions (and subtractions) are done. So `age3 / 3` would be evaluated first, then `age1 + age2`, etc.

3.3.3 Manipulating Text

So far all of the calculations have involved numbers, since that's usually what we think of when we apply math operations like addition. But Java supports two text data types – one for single characters and another for any-length text. Are there operations that are meaningful for those?

Actually, any-length text can be manipulated in several ways using Java. Text stored in two separate variables can be combined, one after the other – this is called "concatenation". Text operations can be done on an any-length text variable with any other variable or value.

For example, consider the declared text variable `String s = "Hello";`. The expression `s + "World"` *joins* two text values – the result is HelloWorld, without a separating space. For there to be a space, the expression would have to be `s + " World"` or `s + " " + "World"` instead.

Java allows the second value in a concatenation expression to be of *any* data type -- it converts it to text before concatenating it.

Another manipulation of any-length text is getting its size by counting the number of letters (and spaces and punctuation) in the text. The expression is `s.length()`, which returns as a whole number the size of the text variable `s`.

Here's an example using text manipulation to create a "form letter":

```
Example: A Form Letter [FormLtr.java]

public class FormLtr
{
    public static void main(String[] argv)
    {
        String name = "George Washington";
        String s = "Congratulations, ";
        s = s + name;
        s = s + "! You have been selected to";
        s = s + " receive one of 5 valuable prizes!";
    }
}
```

The above program does not actually produce any *output* – it just builds and stores a text value. In order to get a program to produce output, we have to include "output statements", which are introduced later in this chapter. And then we have to type a "run" statement to actually "execute" the program.

3.3.4 Using Uninitialized Variables

Values must be stored in variables before those variables appear in an expression, or else it will result in a Java compiler *error*.

Compiler *warnings* do not prevent compilation. Compiler *errors* prevent compilation. But if you receive a warning, it means that something is wrong and to expect unpredictable results from your program. So treat warnings as if they were errors, and make corrections as necessary.

Here's an example that generates a compiler error. Note that the compiler indicates the offending line number:

```
[UninitializedVariables.java]

public class UninitializedVariables
{
    public static void main(String[] argv)
    {
        int a;
        int b;
        int c;
        c = a + b;
    }
}
```

```
● ● ●                    rdb — bash — 69×11
Robert-Burns-Mac-Mini-2:rdb rdb3$ javac UninitializedVariables.java
UninitializedVariables.java:8: error: variable a might not have been
initialized
    c = a + b;
        ^
UninitializedVariables.java:8: error: variable b might not have been
initialized
    c = a + b;
            ^
2 errors
Robert-Burns-Mac-Mini-2:rdb rdb3$ ▊
```

3.4 Output

By now we can store data, perform calculations, and manipulate text. But without output statements, the program keeps all of this to itself! This section explains how to show output on the console screen.

There are 2 output statements in Java,
`System.out.print();` and

`System.out.println();`. It turns out that
`System.out` is an "object" in Java -- the first of which we have
encountered. Any expression, variable, or number that you put
inside the parentheses will appear on the display monitor, below
the command that runs your program. The difference between the
two statements is that the first one does *not* skip to the next line
after outputting, while the second one does. (By the way, that's
"print-el-en", not "print-one-en".)

Output statements can be concatenated like
text, so that you could do something like this:
`System.out.println("My name is " + name);`,
as an alternative to having multiple "print" statements ending with
a "println";

Here are the averaging and form letter examples from above, with
output added:

Complete Example: Average Age [`AvgAge.java`]

```java
public class AvgAge
{
  public static void main(String[] argv)
  {
    int age1 = 19;
    int age2 = 21;
    int age3 = 30;
    int averageAge;

    averageAge = age1 + age2;
    averageAge = averageAge + age3;
    averageAge = averageAge / 3;

    System.out.print("The average age is ");
    System.out.println(averageAge);
  }
}
```

Complete Example: Form Letter [`FormLtr2.cpp`]

```
public class FormLtr2
{
   public static void main(String[] argv)
   {
      String name = "George Washington";

      String s = "Congratulations, ";
      s = s + name;
      s = s + "! You have been selected";
      s = s + "! to receive one of 5";
      s = s + " valuable prizes!";

      System.out.println(s);
   }
}
```

3.4.1 Showing Variables' Values On The Console Screen, *With Labels*

Programmers usually do not output just a variable's value all by itself, like this:

```
System.out.println(age);
```

...because it is difficult to read and understand it on the console screen. In this case, the output could be something like "21" – how does the user of your program know what "21" means, especially if the values of other variables are also shown?

It is better to label your output, so that it looks something like this: "my age is 21" instead of just "21". To include a label in an output statement with one variable, use a statement like this:

Output: Variable With A Label

```
System.out.println("my age is " + age);
```

Note the space at the end of the text in quotes (after the word "is") – it separates the label from the variable's value in the console screen output.

When sending a variable's value to the console screen, be sure to put the *variable's name* in the output statement. Do *not* put its *value*. For example:

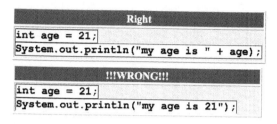

Yes, both result in the same output, but from a maintenance standpoint, the "wrong" way is more difficult to maintain. For example, if you want to change the program next year so that it outputs "22", you would have to change it every place it appears in your program, and each change offers an opportunity for a typing error. But in the "right" way, you just change "21" to "22" in one place, and rest of the program picks up the change automatically and reliably.

3.4.2 A Complete Example: Variables, Values, And Calculations
Here is a program that takes a recipe for one cup of hot chocolate, and multiplies it to serve 8:

Complete Example: Recipe Ingredients Converter [HotChocolate.java]

```java
public class HotChocolate
{
  public static void main(String[] argv)
  {
    double cupsOfMilk = 0.83;
    double vanillaBeans = 0.25;
    double cinnamonSticks = 0.5;
    double ouncesOfChocolate = 0.75;

    double iWantThisManyCups = 8;

    cupsOfMilk = cupsOfMilk * iWantThisManyCups;
    vanillaBeans = vanillaBeans * iWantThisManyCups;
    cinnamonSticks = cinnamonSticks * iWantThisManyCups;
    ouncesOfChocolate = ouncesOfChocolate * iWantThisManyCups;

    System.out.println();
    System.out.println("Recipe for " + iWantThisManyCups + " hot chocolates");
    System.out.println("-----------------------------------------------");
    System.out.println("Cups of milk: " + cupsOfMilk);
    System.out.println("Vanilla beans: " + vanillaBeans);
    System.out.println("Cinnamon sticks: " + cinnamonSticks);
    System.out.println("Ounces of chocolate: " + ouncesOfChocolate);
    System.out.println();
  }
```

3.5 Exercises, Sample Code, Videos, And Addendums

Go to www.rdb3.com/java/3 for extended materials pertaining to this chapter.

Chapter 4. Doing The Math: Libraries

Some problems are too difficult to solve with math operations only – for example, simple amortization. If you deposit $100 each month for 10 years, earning 7.5% interest per year compounded monthly, how much would you have at the end of those 10 years? Here's the formula for this (yikes!):

$$S = D\left(\frac{(1+p)^T - 1}{p}\right)$$

D is the deposit amount of $100 per month, S is the sum at the end of 10 years, p is the *monthly* interest rate (0.075 / 12), and T is the number of months in 10 years (10 * 12). All of this we can do with simple math operations, except for the part about raising something to the power of T. Actually, we could write 120 identical multiplication expressions, but there's got to be a better way! To solve this, we use the built-in math "library"! It contains useful expressions, like raise to a power, find the square root, trig, and exponentials. For example, to raise "x" to the power of "y", use this expression: `Math.pow(x, y)`. `x` and `y` can be any numeric type.

Java programmers refer to `Math.pow(x, y)` as a "function call". Function names follow the same naming rules as variables, which involve the concept of "identifiers". Since identifiers identify both variables and functions, it makes it difficult to tell whether an identifier refers to a variable or a function. But there is an easy way to tell the difference – function calls always have *parentheses*, even if the parentheses are "empty" like they are in `s.length()`, which we saw in the previous chapter.

Here are some handy math functions that work with any numeric types of values and variables:

math operation	In Java
square root	`Math.sqrt(x)`
sine	`Math.sin(x)`
cosine	`Math.cos(x)`
raise "e" to a power	`Math.exp(x)`
raise "x" to the power "y"	`Math.pow(x, y)`

"Libraries" add functionality to a computer language – they add features that are not part of the base language. Think of them as expansion modules, like you might buy for a board game like "Settlers of Catan, Traders and Barbarians Expansion", or for a computer game like the "Halo 4 Multiplayer Map Pack". A feature to raise a number to a power is actually *not* part of the base Java computer language – it's in the "java.math" expansion library. But the use of **Math.pow** and other math functions is so common that the java.math expansion library is included automatically with Java – you don't have to do a thing to attach it.

So here's the amortization calculation for an *annual* interest rate of 7.5% – make sure you understand the conversion of annual interest rate as a percent to monthly interest rate in decimal:

Example: Amortization Calculation [`AmortizationCalc.java`]

```
public class AmortizationCalc
{
  public static void main(String[] argv)
  {
    // assignment upon declaration (see 3.2.3)
    double D = 100;
    double p = 0.075 / 12;
    double T = 10 * 12;

    // the pow subprogram (new)
    double S = D * ((Math.pow(1 + p, T) - 1) / p);
  }
}
```

Of course, there is an infinite number of ways to write the above code, including the choice of variable names and the use of one complex expression versus using several simpler expressions. Actually the variable names do not even conform to the convention of starting with lowercase letters. This deviation from convention was done to match the variables in the original equation, and this is an acceptable practice.

Also, note the use of `//` in the above example. These denote "comments" – programmer's notes that are included in code but are ignored by the compiler. They are used throughout the rest of this book to refer back to other parts of the book where certain code structures were first introduced.

4.1 Whole Number Division And Truncation

The division operation often results in a fractional part in the answer. Our average age example above ended in `70 / 3`, which has a fractional part when resolved. But there is an inherent inconsistency when using division with whole numbers, because whole numbers cannot have fractional parts. To solve this, Java simply throws away, or *truncates* any fractional value. It does not round to the nearest – it truncates. So `99 / 100` resolves to zero!

Note that when using numbers in calculations, whole numbers without decimals are treated as whole numbers, and numbers with decimals are treated as floating point numbers!

A classic problem in programming is the conversion of temperature from Celsius to Fahrenheit. The formula is f = (9 / 5) * c + 32. If we were to program this as `f = (9 / 5) * c + 32;`, we would have a problem because `9 / 5` resolves to one! But if either of the 2 numbers in an operation is a floating point number, then the operation is resolved as if both were floating point. So one solution is to write the statement this way: `f = (9.0 / 5) * c + 32;` . And it really does not matter how "c" is declared – whole number or floating point – because it gets multiplied by the floating point result, 1.8 (that is, 9.0/5), and is thus temporarily "promoted" to floating point for purposes of the calculation.

In fact, to help avoid problems like this, Java does not allow the floating point result of an expression to be assigned to an integer variable!

4.1.1 Who Are You, Anyway?

Did you see how `f` and `c` just got used in the previous code samples without any introduction? You can probably guess that these are variable names. But we know Java compilers are a bit more formal – they require an introduction in the form of a declaration statement before they will deal with `f` and `c`. So we can presume that somewhere *before* they get used in the conversion calculation there's a `double f;` statement and a `double c;` statement, so that they are formally introduced to the compiler.

4.1.2 Not A Clue

Wouldn't you think that `f = 9 / 5;` would store the value 1.8 into the variable `f`? After all, `f` is declared as a floating point variable and that should be a clue for the compiler to know what to do. But here's the thing – the whole expression to the *right* of the `=` sign gets evaluated *before* the compiler even looks at the variable name on the left! So as was already said, `9 / 5` resolves to one. *Then* that result gets stored in the variable. Truncation already happened.

4.2 Formatting Output

Computer calculations are accurate. They are so accurate that computers feel they have to show all the digits behind the decimal. Consider `10.0 / 3` – the result is 3.33333333333333.... The computer likes to show all the 3's that it has, up to Java's default limit of 15 or so total digits. But you can force the computer to round off numbers and show them with a desired number of digits after the decimal. Here's how:

First, use this statement at the top of the code: `import java.text.*;` to attach the "java.text" expansion library -- which you do *not* get automatically with Java! (Actually, it does not really *cost* anything, other than that you have to type the import statement.) If you have more than one import statement for additional libraries, they can follow one another and the order does not matter. Then for a floating point number declared as `double x;`, print the number like this: `System.out.print(new DecimalFormat("#.00").format(x));` instead of `System.out.print(x);` to get 2 decimal digits.

Note that formatting applies only to the *appearance* of a number when it appears in the output. It does *not* affect its actual value as stored in the program's memory.

Here's the amortization calculation, with *formatted output*. Normally we do not apply formatting to *echoes* of input values – *echo* means to send an *input* value to output.

Complete Example: Amortization Calculation [`AmortizationCalc2.java`]

```
import java.text.*;

public class AmortizationCalc2
{
  public static void main(String[] argv)
  {
    // input values
    double years = 10;
    double D = 100;

    // output (calculated) values
    double p = 0.075 / 12;
    double T = years * 12;
    double S = D * ((Math.pow(1 + p, T) - 1) / p);

    // echoing input values, unformatted
    System.out.print("In " + years + " years, $");
    System.out.print(D);
    System.out.print(" deposited per month will grow to $");

    // formatting output (see 4.2)
    System.out.print(new DecimalFormat("#,000.00").format(S));
    System.out.println(".");
  }
}
```

Note that a new variable was introduced: **years**. It is used in the calculation of **T**, but the real reason that it is specified separately is that it is included in the output statement. An alternative is to simply repeat the **10** in the output statement, but then the number

would appear twice, and that is *not good programming practice*!
What if you wanted to change the program for 8 years instead of
10? You'd have to find it and change it twice, which invites errors
of typing and of omission.

Also note the import at the top of the code listing. It attaches the
"java.text" library to the program, so that `DecimalFormat`
can be used.

There are many ways to have constructed the output sequence. The
main reason for doing it the way it is done above is to fit it on a
page nicely, but it also shows the variety of ways that expressions
can be combined.

Copy, compile, and run this example. The result should be "In 10
years, $100 deposited per month will grow to $17793.03". To put
this into perspective, putting $100 per month into a piggy bank for
10 years would amount to $12,000, because there is zero interest in
piggy banks.

4.2.1 Code Blocks
Usually it takes more that a single statement to do one thing in a
program. For example, the output section at the end of the Java
sample program **AmortizationCalc2.java** requires 5 statements
to complete. Similarly in written language it can take several
sentences to complete a thought. In written English we use
paragraphs to group related sentences together to form a thought.
In programming we use *code blocks*.

Code blocks are written in programs purely for organizational
purposes. Their use, correct or otherwise, has no impact on a
program's operation.

Code blocks usually contain a comment line that explains the
purpose of the code block, so that a reader of the program does
not have to read all the statements in the code block in order to
figure out what it does. Short code blocks do not always need a
comment line, if they are easy to read and understand. To make
code blocks easier to spot in a long program, skipped lines usually

separate them. Here is what the output code block looks like with a comment line:

```
A Code Block With A Comment Label
// summarize input and calculated values
System.out.print("In " + new DecimalFormat("#").format(years) + " years, $");
System.out.print(new DecimalFormat("#").format(D));
System.out.print(" deposited per month will grow to $");
System.out.print(new DecimalFormat("#,000.00").format(S));
System.out.println(".");
```

Code blocks with comment labels are used throughout the remainder of this book.

4.3 More Handy Libraries And Functions

Besides libraries for math and formatting, most computer languages have many additional libraries with functions that perform complex operations that would be difficult for us to duplicate with the simple math operations supported by the language. Here are some of them:

Some More Handy Java Library Functions	
function call	Explanation
Character.toUpperCase(x)	uppercase char version of x, where x is a char
Character.toLowerCase(x)	lowercase char version of x, where x is a char
Math.abs(x)	absolute value of x, where x is an integer or floating point number

It's important to remember that these function calls do *not* change the value of **x**. They simply *resolve* to that version of **x** for use in whatever statement contains the expression.

4.3.1 Conversion Statements

The Java function calls in the above table are all *expressions*. They are not stand-alone *statements* – it's important to understand the difference! They resolve to *new* values – they do not modify the original value stored in the variable **x**. In order to change a stored value, you need to use an expression in an assignment statement, as in these examples:

Some Handy Java Conversion Statements	
statement	**Explanation**
`x = Character.toUpperCase(x);`	uppercase char version of x, where x is a char
`x = Character.toLowerCase(x);`	lowercase char version of x, where x is a char
`x = Math.abs(x);`	absolute value of x, where x is an integer or floating point number

Note that `Character.toUpperCase` and `Character.toLowerCase` work only for `char` values and variables. They do *not* work for `String` values or variables. A way for converting the case of a `String` will be presented in chapter 6.

4.3.2 Using Multiple `import` Statements

Many programs attach more than one library in separate `import` statements. You will be seeing some of these in later chapters. The order of appearance of the libraries does not matter. But a convention is used in this book that makes it easier to deal with long lists of such statements: *put the libraries in alphabetical order*. Following this convention makes the libraries easier to track in your Java files.

4.4 Exercises, Sample Code, Videos, And Addendums

Go to www.rdb3.com/java/4 for extended materials pertaining to this chapter.

Chapter 5. Interactive Programs: Console I/O

Input can be gathered from a variety of sources. In chapters 3 and 4 we specified input values directly in the program source code. That worked fine, but if we wanted to use different input, such as changing the number of years in the amortization calculation, the program had to be edited and recompiled. That is certainly not the kind of program that you could distribute for non-programmers to use!

It would be nice if the program could *prompt* (or ask) the user to type input values on the keyboard, and transfer those values into the variables in the program. Then we could develop and compile the program only once, and it could be applied to a virtually unlimited range of input values.

This is what *interactive* programs do. They are designed for a certain amount of interaction to take place between the user and the program. This interaction transfers data values into variables, *after* the program has been written and compiled!

5.1 Capturing Values From The Keyboard

Capturing input from the keyboard involves three steps, which have to be represented in code:

3 Steps For Keyboard Input
1. Declare a variable in the computer's memory to store the input value.
2. Prompt the user to type an input value and press the ENTER key.
3. Transfer the keyboard entry into the variable declared for this use.

Here is a simple example:

```
Simple Example Of Console I/O [YourAge.java]

import java.io.*;

public class YourAge
{
  public static void main(String[] argv) throws Exception
  {
    BufferedReader cin;
    cin = new BufferedReader(new InputStreamReader(System.in));

    // a code block to read an int value from the keyboard
    int age;                                          // step 1
    System.out.print("What is your age? ");           // step 2
    age = new Double(cin.readLine()).intValue();      // step 3
  }
}
```

It looks pretty complicated, but it's not as bad as it seems. Let's break it down. First, the program has to be told that we will be using the computer's *console* (that is, the keyboard and the display monitor). That's what `import java.io.*;` does in Java. There is a `BufferedReader cin;` statement and another following it. It turns out that `cin` is an "object", the second of which we have encountered so far. It's pronounced, "see in" and stands for "console input". We could actually name it whatever we wish, but this matches the same object in C++ that also goes by that name.

This next sample program includes code blocks for each of the data types we have studied so far. Unlike the previous example, there are no output statements to echo the entered values to the console screen:

Transferring Values From The Keyboard [ItsAboutYou.java]

```java
import java.io.*;

public class ItsAboutYou
{
   public static void main(String[] argv) throws Exception
   {
      BufferedReader cin;
      cin = new BufferedReader(new InputStreamReader(System.in));

      // read an int value from the keyboard
      int age;
      System.out.print("What is your age? ");
      age = new Double(cin.readLine()).intValue();

      // read a double value from the keyboard
      double gpa;
      System.out.print("What is your grade point average? ");
      gpa = new Double(cin.readLine()).doubleValue();

      // read a String value from the keyboard
      String name;
      System.out.print("What is your name? ");
      name = cin.readLine();

      // read a char value from the keyboard
      char gender;
      System.out.print("What is your gender? [M/F]: ");
      gender = cin.readLine().charAt(0);
   }
}
```

Note the **import** for using the **cin** object. Then there are four separate examples of keyboard input in the above code blocks – one for a whole number, one for a floating point number, and two for text. They are entirely independent of each other, and can be used in any combination to match the needs of your program. Each follows the three steps: (1) variable declaration, (2) user prompt, and (3) transfer of data from the keyboard to the variable. The variable declaration does not have to be immediately before the prompt – it just has to be somewhere before the transfer statement. The prompt (with a **System.out.print**) alerts the user that the computer is waiting for something to be typed on the keyboard and the ENTER key pressed. Note that the prompts are enclosed in quotes (so it's hard to have a quote as part of the prompt itself!) Prompts are not required, but it's hard for a user to know what to do without them. It would be like staring at someone and waiting for them to answer, without you having asked a question!

Note that each Java code block consists of a single *assignment statement*, but instead of assigning a specific value, it transfers a value from the keyboard using a rather complicated expression. Each one includes the expression `cin.readLine()` which reads a `String`, but is otherwise unique to the data type.

Use these code blocks to add keyboard input to your programs by copying, pasting, and adapting the sample code! (To adapt the code, change the variable names and prompts to suit your program.)

5.2 Prompts

The statements with `cin` in them cause the program to pause and wait for the user to press the ENTER key before continuing. Program execution actually suspends there, waiting for the ENTER key to be pressed. Anything that is typed before the ENTER key gets pressed is then captured by the program, and can be stored in a variable. If nothing gets typed, the user gets another chance to enter something – *anything* – before pressing ENTER again.

But on the computer screen, the only evidence of the `cin` statement is a flashing symbol – usually a horizontal line. This is not very much of a clue for the user to know that something is supposed to be typed now, followed by the ENTER key. So `cin` is usually preceded by a `System.out.print` with instructions for the user. This is called a *prompt*.

The following shows how a program would work without, and with, a prompt.

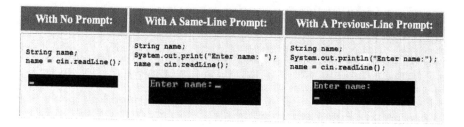

With No Prompt:	With A Same-Line Prompt:	With A Previous-Line Prompt:

`String name;`
`name = cin.readLine();`
	`String name;`
	`System.out.print("Enter name: ");`
	`name = cin.readLine();`
		`String name;`
		`System.out.println("Enter name:");`
		`name = cin.readLine();`

	Enter name:	Enter name:

There are two ways to place the prompt: either on the same line where the user input is to be typed, or on the previous line. Both ways are shown above, but the same-line prompt is used in most of the example programs in this book. Note that the same-line prompt includes a separating space at the end of the prompt message (after the colon): **"Enter name: "**, but the previous-line prompt does not: **"Enter name:"**. Also, it is common to include possible responses in the prompt, enclosed in square brackets and separated by commas or slashes, like this: **"What is your gender? [M/F]: "**, as a guide to the user.

Unless you have a very good reason to do otherwise, *always* have a prompt for *each* user-entered value. Every time you expect the user to type something and press ENTER, or just to press ENTER after a pause, do this: precede it with a same-line or previous-line prompt, so that the user knows to do something. And if you can include some guidance, such as possible responses or an example response, do so.

5.3 Interrupting An Interactive Program

Sometimes in the process of writing and testing a program that has console input, it may be convenient to terminate (that is, end or exit) a program early. For example, if the input involves a series of prompts, you may notice incorrect spelling in the first prompt. In order to stop right away and fix it, rather than continue on through the remaining prompts and normal termination of the program, you can type CTRL-C to make the program stop. On a PC, hold down the *CTRL* (or *control*) key, press the letter C key, and then release both. On a Mac, it's the *control* key and the C key.

5.4 Exercises, Sample Code, Videos, And Addendums

Go to www.rdb3.com/java/5 for extended materials pertaining to this chapter.

PART 2: Programming Logic

Chapter 6. Simple Logic: Basic Branching/Looping
6.1 The If-Statement
6.2 Comparison Operators
6.3 True/False If-Statements
6.4 Curly-Brace Containers
6.5 The While-True Loop
6.6 The While-True-If-Break Loop
6.7 Bringing It All Together: Programming With Logic
6.8 Classic Computer Science Solutions That Use Logic
6.9 Exercises, Sample Code, Videos, And Addendums

Chapter 7. More Than One Way: Advanced Branching/Looping
7.1 Multiple Choice If-Statements
7.2 Event-Controlled vs Count-Controlled Loops
7.3 Introducing The For-Loop
7.4 Nested Loops
7.5 Four Forms Of The If-Statement
7.6 Four Forms Of Loops
7.7 Advanced Logic Considerations
7.8 Exercises, Sample Code, Videos, And Addendums

Chapter 8. Simplifying Complicated Programs Using Functions
8.1 Value-Returning Functions
8.2 Parameter Lists
8.3 Void Functions
8.4 Some Examples With Functions
8.5 Classic Computer Science Solutions
8.6 Exercises, Sample Code, Videos, And Addendums

Chapter 9. Counting On Your Fingers: Bits And Bytes
9.1 Computer Memory: Vast Arrays Of On/Off Switches
9.2 Floating Point Numbers
9.3 Representing Characters
9.4 The True/False, Yes/No, On/Off, Up/Down, Left/Right Data Type
9.5 Literal Values
9.6 Type Casting
9.7 Exercises, Sample Code, Videos, And Addendums

Chapter 10. Interactive Programs: File I/O
10.1 Text File Input
10.2 Text File Output
10.3 Exercises, Sample Code, Videos, And Addendums

Chapter 6. Simple Logic: Basic Branching/Looping

As shown in chapter 1, branching and looping are ways to make programs more interesting and useful by allowing them to skip and jump around among statements, rather than follow a strict sequence from top to bottom, with no options. The decision points in programs where the flow of the program can either continue in a sequence or skip to somewhere else involves "logic" – something like, "if this condition exists, then do something – otherwise, skip over that something".

6.1 The If-Statement

In both of the following examples, the *indented* output statement gets executed *only* if the user's guess is correct. This is the basic "if-statement" for use in branching – it allows branching *over* the indented statement.

```
Using Branching Logic [OneToTen.java]

import java.io.*;

public class OneToTen
{
    public static void main(String[] argv) throws Exception
    {
        BufferedReader cin;
        cin = new BufferedReader(new InputStreamReader(System.in));

        // read a score from the keyboard (see 5.1)
        int usersGuess;
        System.out.println("I am thinking of a number between 1-10");
        System.out.print("Try to guess the number [1-10]: ");
        usersGuess = new Double(cin.readLine()).intValue();

        // see if the guess is right
        if (usersGuess == 7)
            System.out.println("You guessed it!");
    }
}
```

More Branching Logic [Rumpelstiltskin.java]

```java
import java.io.*;

public class Rumpelstiltskin
{
  public static void main(String[] argv) throws Exception
  {
    BufferedReader cin;
    cin = new BufferedReader(new InputStreamReader(System.in));

    // read text from the keyboard (see 5.1)
    String usersGuess;
    System.out.println("Try to guess my name: ");
    usersGuess = cin.readLine();

    // see if the guess is right
    if (usersGuess.equalsIgnoreCase("Rumpelstiltskin"))
      System.out.println("Argh!!!");
    System.out.println("GOODBYE");
  }
}
```

These if-statements begin with the lowercase word **if**. Inside its parentheses, values and variables are compared to see if the are equal. If so, the next line gets included, otherwise not. That odd-looking, two-character symbol is double-equals, **==**. It tells the program to compare based on equality. Double-equals does not work for **String**s the way you think it would – that's why it's done a different way above.

Note that there is no semicolon at the end of the `if (...)` statements, like there is with other Java statements. Compilers allow you to put semicolons there, so you have to remember this for yourself!

In the second program, GOODBYE gets sent to output no matter what – only one line, the indented one, belongs to the if-statement. But as we'll learn later, it's not the indenting that's important in Java – it's something else. We'll get to that soon enough.

6.2 Comparison Operators

Along with `==`, there are six commonly used "operators". An operator is something that uses the values and/or variables next to it and does something with them. The following table lists some operators that *compare* values and variables:

Some Comparison Operator Symbols	
>	is greater than
<	is less than
>=	is greater than or equal to
<=	is less than or equal to
==	is equal to
!=	is not equal to

The symbols for some of these operators consist of *two characters*. They should be typed without being separated by spaces. When an operator is typed with two numbers, variables, or expressions on either side of it, the result is a *simple logical expression*, like `number == 7`. There are single spaces separating the operator symbol from the two items it compares – these are not required, but are there for readability.

Here are some examples of simple logical expressions, which could be placed inside the parentheses of an if-statement:

Examples Of Logical Expressions, Using Comparison Operators	
`x < 10`	tests whether the value stored in x is less than 10 (x must be an already-declared whole number or floating point variable)
`a != b`	tests whether a and b have different values (a and b must be variables of the same data type: both whole numbers, both floating points, both characters, but *not* `String`s
`gender == 'F'`	tests whether gender is F (gender must be a single-character data type variable, `char`)

It is important to remember that the test for equality has *two* back-to-back equal signs. You may recall that a single equal sign already means something: assignment of a value to a variable. So a different symbol is needed for the equality operator.

Comparisons involving text *values* are done differently for single-character text (**char**s) than for text of any length (**String**s). *Single*-character variables have to be compared using *single* quote marks around the character (like **'F'**). Text of *any length* needs to be contained inside *double* quotes (like **"Hello"**) and they need to be compared like this – *without* using operators:

Examples Of Comparing Strings	
s.equals("Hello")	tests whether the text stored in **s** is exactly equal to "Hello", with matching letter case (**s** must be a Java **String** variable).
s.equalsIgnoreCase("Hello")	tests whether the text stored in **s** is equal to "Hello", "hello", "HeLlO", regardless of the letters' case.
!s.equals("Hello")	tests whether the text stored in **s** is *not* exactly equal to "Hello".
!s.equalsIgnoreCase ("Hello")	tests whether the text stored in **s** is *not* equal to "Hello", regardless of the letters' case.

6.2.1 This AND That

Sometimes it is convenient to test for a range of values, or test for more than one possible value of a variable. For that reason, most computer languages let you put multiple logical expressions together in such a way that the *all* have to be satisfied in order for the if-statement to evaluate to true. Here's an example: "if the test score is greater or equal to 80, *and* less than 90, then assign a grade of B." Here's an example: "if the score is 80-89, the student's grade is B."

the algorithm for and-logic:
read a score from the keyboard as a whole number
if the score is 80 or greater AND less than 90
    output "grade B"

```
                    Using And-Logic [GradeB.java]

import java.io.*;

public class GradeB
{
  public static void main(String[] argv) throws Exception
  {
    BufferedReader cin;
    cin = new BufferedReader(new InputStreamReader(System.in));

    // read a score from the keyboard (see 5.1)
    int score;
    System.out.print("What is your test score? [0-100]: ");
    score = new Double(cin.readLine()).intValue();

    // see if score is in the B range
    if (score >= 80 && score < 90)
      System.out.println("Your grade is B");
  }
}
```

The symbol that joins two (or more) simple logical expressions with "and-logic" is **&&**, and the result is a "compound logical expression". Note the single spaces surrounding the symbol – they are not required, but are there for readability. Also note that there is repetition in the if-statement – **score** is typed twice. There is no way to say "if the score is greater than or equal to 80 and less than 90" in Java. You have to say "if the score is greater than or equal to 80 *and* the score less than 90" instead.

It might not make any difference to you now, but the computer does not always need to evaluate all of the simple logical expressions when using and-logic. For example, if the score is 50, the "greater than or equal to 80" part is false, so there is no point in checking if "the score less than 90".

6.2.2 This OR That

It's also possible to combine multiple logical expressions such that *any one* has to be satisfied in order for the if-statement to evaluate to true. The following example shows how to use "or-logic": "if the grade is A, B, or C, the student passes the class":

the algorithm for or-logic:
read a grade from the keyboard as a single letter
if the grade is uppercase A, B, or C
    output "you pass"

```
                  Using Or-Logic [PassingGrade.java]

import java.io.*;

public class PassingGrade
{
  public static void main(String[] argv) throws Exception
  {
    BufferedReader cin;
    cin = new BufferedReader(new InputStreamReader(System.in));

    // read a grade from the keyboard (see 5.1)
    char grade;
    System.out.print("What is your grade? [A, B, C, D, or F]: ");
    grade = cin.readLine().charAt(0);

    // check for passing grade
    if (grade == 'A' || grade == 'B' || grade == 'C')
      System.out.println("You pass");
  }
}
```

The symbol that joins two (or more) simple logical expressions with or-logic is ||. (This is not a commonly typed symbol outside of programming – it's usually the SHIFT-BACKSLASH keystroke.) Note the single spaces surrounding the symbol – they are not required, but are there for readability. Also note that there is repetition in the statement – **grade** is typed three times. You do not say "if the grade is A or B or C" in code. You say, "if the grade is A *or* the grade is B *or* the grade is C" instead.

Again, computers do not always need to evaluate all of the simple logical expressions in or-logic. For example, if the grade is A, the "grade is A" part is true, so there is no point in checking if the "grade is B" or if the "grade is C".

6.2.3 This AND That OR That OR Something Else
Be careful – it is possible to join simple logical expressions with **&&**s and ||s all in the same if-statement. But this is usually not a good idea, because the exact meaning of the

logic can be confusing. It has to do with the order in which operations are evaluated, left to right. For example, don't do `score >= 0 && score < 80 || score >= 90 && score <= 100` to test for scores that are not B. But you can force the order of evaluation of the logical expressions using parentheses like this: `(score >= 0 && score < 80) || (score >= 90 && score <= 100)`! Inside an if-statement, it would look like this – note the "nested" parentheses: `if ((score >= 0 && score < 80) || (score >= 90 && score <= 100))`.

Also note that the variable that appears multiple times in complex logical expressions does not have to be the same variable in each of the simple logical expressions. You can do this, for example: `score > 86 && grade == 'B'` to test for a high B.

6.2.4 Handling "Case"

What if the prompt for grade tells the user to enter an uppercase letter grade, but the user types a lowercase letter instead? After all, the letters are shown in uppercase on console keyboard keys! Rather than not recognize "a" as "A", you can do one of two things: check for either case, or *temporarily* convert case before checking the value. For example:

`grade == 'A' || grade == 'a'`
or
`Character.toUpperCase(grade) == 'A'`

6.3 True/False If-Statements

Often it is convenient to use logic to switch between two possible code blocks – one if a comparison is true, and another if it's false. This is possible using two different if-statements with opposite comparison expressions in their parentheses, but an easier way is to append an `else` clause to the end of the if-statement, thereby applying "if-else logic". Here's an example:

the algorithm for if-else logic:
read a grade from the keyboard as a single letter
if the grade is uppercase A, B, or C
    output "you pass"
otherwise
    output "you don't pass"

Using If-Else Logic [`PassNoPass.java`]

```java
import java.io.*;

public class PassNoPass
{
    public static void main(String[] argv) throws Exception
    {
        BufferedReader cin;
        cin = new BufferedReader(new InputStreamReader(System.in));

        // read a grade from the keyboard (see 5.1)
        char grade;
        System.out.print("What is your grade? [A, B, C, D, or F]: ");
        grade = cin.readLine().charAt(0);

        if (grade == 'A' || grade == 'B' || grade == 'C')
            System.out.println("You pass");
        else
            System.out.println("You do not pass");
    }
}
```

The **else** is followed by another output statement to be used
if the expression in the if-statement's parentheses evaluates to
false. Note that **else** cannot be used in Java unless it follows an
if-statement.

6.4 Curly-Brace Containers

Up to now, the if-statements we've considered have all been
associated with single output statements. That is, if the expression
in the if-statement's parentheses evaluates to true, then execute
the following indented statement. But what if you want to execute
more than one statement? You could try adding them and indenting
them, too, but that does not work in Java like you'd expect. Only
the *first* statement, indented or not, belongs to the if-statement. All
the others are treated as if they were not indented at all.

To include multiple lines, put them in a *curly-brace container* and put that right below the if-statement (or below the `else`) instead of one indented statement. It's still a good idea to indent all the statements inside the container anyway, but only because it's easier for humans to read. Here's an example:

```
           The Curly-Brace Container
if (score >= 90)
{
   cout << "Your grade is A" << endl;
   numberOfAs = numberOfAs + 1;
}
```

See how the opening and closing curly-brace symbols align vertically directly under the "i" in "if"? It's not required that they line up like this, and some programmers do this differently, but doing so does make the source code more human-friendly.

6.5 The While-True Loop

The if-statement implements branching; the *while-true loop* implements looping back. Loops consist of statements that are to be repeated by looping from *after* the last statement, back up to *before* the first. Each pass through a loop is called a "cycle".

A while-true loop begins with the `while (true)` statement followed by a curly-brace container – just like the ones used with if-statements and introduced earlier in this chapter. Here's an example:

```
             The While-True Loop
while (true)
{
   the 1st statement in the loop
   another statement in the loop
   . . .
   another statement in the loop
   the last statement in the loop
}
```

Note that there is no semicolon at the end of the
`while (true)` statement – same as `if (...)` . The word
"while" is separated from the first parenthesis by a space, but this is
not required. Here is a modification to **PassingGrade.java** program
from earlier in this chapter, which now allows an unlimited number
of repeats in what programmers call an "infinite loop".

the algorithm for an infinite loop:
```
loop starts here
    get user's grade via keyboard
    if A, B, or C
        output "you pass"
loop back from here
```

An Infinite Loop [`PassingGradeL.java`]

```java
import java.io.*;

public class PassingGradeL
{
  public static void main(String[] argv) throws Exception
  {
    BufferedReader cin;
    cin = new BufferedReader(new InputStreamReader(System.in));

    while (true)
    {
      char grade; // read a char value from the keyboard (see 5.1)
      System.out.print("What is your grade? [A, B, C, D, or F]: ");
      grade = cin.readLine().charAt(0);

      if (grade == 'A' || grade == 'B' || grade == 'C') // see 6.2.2
        System.out.println("You pass");
    }
  }
}
```

This loops over and over, actually never ending! The way out of
this loop is to press CTRL-C (or control-C) instead of typing a
grade when prompted. There really should be a prompt that tells
the user to "Use CTRL-C to quit...". But relying on CTRL-C to end
a program is really not good programming practice. We come up
with a better way in the next section.

Note however that the only difference between the above program
and its predecessor is insertion of the looping code, and indenting

of the code block. So looping is *very easy* to implement in Java code.

6.5.1 Infinite Loops

As already mentioned, what we created in the above example is called an infinite loop, because it repeats over and over, to infinity. There is no way to end the program normally. CTRL-C (or control-C) ends it, but it ends the *program*, not just the loop. If there were any more code after the loop to be processed, it would be skipped upon CTRL-C (or control-C).

You don't want your program to get stuck in an infinite loop. You need to design a way out of the loop that does not kill the program, and that's where the "if-break" statement comes in.

6.6 The While-True-If-Break Loop

The purpose of *if-break* is to define a condition under which looping would discontinue, and sequential processing would pick up at the first statement *after* the loop's curly-brace container. For example, the user could enter a grade of X to indicate that the **PassingGradeL.java** program should stop looping and skip to the end. Adding one or more if-break statements to a while-true loop gives you a while-true-if-break loop, with a way out of the loop that does not kill the program. Here's an example:

```
The While-True-If-Break Loop
while (true)
{
    ...
    if (...) break;
    ...
}
```

For example, after reading the grade in the above example, you could add the statement `if (grade == 'X') break;` . Of course, you need to let the user know about this feature, so the prompt may change to something like this:

"What is your grade? [A, B, C, D, F, or X to quit]: ". It would look something like this:

the algorithm for a not-so-infinite loop:

```
loop starts here
    get user's grade via keyboard
    if X break
    if A, B, or C
        output "you pass"
    loop back from here
output "thanks"
```

A Not-So-Infinite Loop [PassingGradeIB.java]

```java
import java.io.*;

public class PassingGradeIB
{
  public static void main(String[] argv) throws Exception
  {
    BufferedReader cin;
    cin = new BufferedReader(new InputStreamReader(System.in));

    while (true)
    {
      char grade;
      System.out.print("What is your grade? [A, B, C, D, F, or X to quit]: ");
      grade = cin.readLine().charAt(0);

      if (grade == 'X' || grade == 'x') break;

      if (grade == 'A' || grade == 'B' || grade == 'C')
        System.out.println("You pass");
    } // while

    System.out.println("Thanks for checking your grades!");
  } // main
} // public class
```

Note the minor enhancement added to this program – it accepts uppercase *or* lowercase X to end the loop. (This is what's known as a *sentinel* – it signifies the end of a process.) The program also sends a thank you note to output before the program ends.

6.6.1 Closing Curly-Brace Comments

Also note that comment labels appear at the end of each closing curly-brace in the previous program sample. As we come up with more and more uses for curly-brace containers, it will become more and more difficult to look at a closing curly-brace and know what it's for. If you are good about always aligning each closing curly with its matching opening curly-brace, and indenting code blocks inside curly-braces, then it will always be possible to find the match to a curly-brace by scrolling through your code. But some programmers also like to label their closing curly-braces, as is done above.

Recall that a double-slash **//** prepended to any line – even blank ones – is an indicator to the compiler to ignore anything that follows on the same line. You can use that space for typing comments, which are usually meant to remind *you* of what you were thinking! This is the first opportunity we've had to include comments for some useful purpose. It's easy to over-comment code and obscure it with comments to the obvious (like `int a; // declare "a" as an int`). So we use them sparingly.

Comments are also used to type identifying information at the top of a program file, with the programmer's name and other identifying information. To save space and to focus attention on the code, these are left out of the sample code listings in this book. But programmers should always use identification comments at the tops of their code listings.

6.7 Bringing It All Together: Programming With Logic

Here are some examples with **if** and **while**. You can copy, save, and compile them. You can modify them and see how they work. Make sure that you understand everything in each of these examples.

6.7.1 Another Infinite Loop
Here is another program with an infinite loop. Note that the prompt instructs the user to press CTRL-C to stop the program.

Another Infinite Loop [TempConvert.java]

```java
import java.io.*;
import java.text.*;

public class TempConvert
{
  public static void main(String[] argv) throws Exception
  {
    BufferedReader cin;
    cin = new BufferedReader(new InputStreamReader(System.in));

    double f; // degrees F
    double c; // degrees C

    while (true)
    {
      System.out.print("Enter temperature in degrees Celsius [CTRL-C to exit]: ")
      c = new Double(cin.readLine()).doubleValue();

      f = 9.0 / 5 * c + 32;
      System.out.print("The temperature in degrees F is ");
      System.out.println(new DecimalFormat("#.0").format(f));
    } // while
  } // main
} // public class
```

In the above example, the variables **c** and **f** could have been declared *inside* the loop, because they are not used after the loop ends and before the program ends. It also uses the ill-advised CTRL-C to exit the loop – see if you can think of a better way to end the program!

6.7.2 A Quiz Program

The following example shows a quiz with one math question (8+2=?). It demonstrates some formatting code, too, so that the prompts are aligned and not fully left justified at the edge of the screen.

the algorithm for a quiz program:
prompt the user with the quiz question for 8 + 2
read the user's answer from the keyboard
if the answer is 10
    output "correct"
otherwise
    output "incorrect"

A Quiz Program [Quiz.java]

```java
import java.io.*;

public class Quiz
{
  public static void main(String[] argv) throws Exception
  {
    BufferedReader cin;
    cin = new BufferedReader(new InputStreamReader(System.in));

    // read an int (see 5.1) using a very lengthy prompt
    int answer;
    System.out.println("\n\n\n");
    System.out.println("        8");
    System.out.println("       +2");
    System.out.println("       --");

    System.out.print("        ");
    answer = new Double(cin.readLine()).intValue();

    System.out.print("        ");
    if (answer == 10)
      System.out.println("Correct!");
    else
      System.out.println("Very good, but a better answer is 10");
  }
}
```

Note the `System.out.println("\n\n\n");`
statement in the Java example. Each **\n** skips one line. Since
there are 3 of them, and since the statement has "println" instead
of "print", four lines are skipped. This is done just to clear some
space.

The output statements contain leading spaces inside the quote
marks – this is to move the "8" and the "+2" over from the
extreme left edge of the console window. The spaces are arranged
so that the "2" in "+2" aligns under the "8" above it. Also note
the statement that contains the two dashes (**--**) looks like the
horizontal line you would draw if you were to write this math
problem on a piece of paper.

6.7.3 Simple While-True-If-Break Loops

Here are some programs that use if-break to exit a loop. Since the
if-break is the very last statement in the loops of both programs, it
offers an opportunity to apply a variation of the while-true loop,

called the "do-while" loop – we'll look at that one in the next chapter.

A Simple Loop [ThereYet.java]

```java
import java.io.*;

public class ThereYet
{
  public static void main(String[] argv) throws Exception
  {
    BufferedReader cin;
    cin = new BufferedReader(new InputStreamReader(System.in));

    while (true)
    {
      String answer;
      System.out.print("Are we there yet? ");
      answer = cin.readLine();
      if (answer.equals("yes")) break;
    } // while
  } // main
} // public class
```

Another Simple Loop [CrossTheRoad.java]

```java
import java.io.*;

public class CrossTheRoad
{
  public static void main(String[] argv) throws Exception
  {
    BufferedReader cin;
    cin = new BufferedReader(new InputStreamReader(System.in));

    System.out.println("Approach the curb.");
    while (true)
    {
      char answer;
      System.out.print("Look both ways. Is it clear [Y/N]? ");

      answer = cin.readLine().charAt(0);

      if (answer == 'Y' || answer == 'y') break;
    } // while

    System.out.println("It's safe to cross");
  } // main
} // public class
```

In the sample above, note that we don't even check for the user to input "N". What's going on is this: "Y" is considered as yes – so is "y". *Anything else* is considered "no". To avoid confusion, it might be better to not accept answers other than "Y" or "N". That's what "validation loops" are for.

6.7.4 Validation Loops

Validation loops are used with console input to make sure the user types valid entries. These loops repeat until a valid value is received, and usually output a message after detecting invalid input and before doing another cycle of the loop. Here is code block that prompts for grades to be entered:

Without Validation

```
char grade;
System.out.print("What is your grade? [A, B, C, D, F, or X to quit]: ");
grade = cin.readLine().charAt(0);
```

With A Validation Loop

```
char grade; // declare above loop in order to use after loop
while (true)
{
    System.out.print("What is your grade? [A, B, C, D, F, or X to quit]: ");
    grade = cin.readLine().charAt(0);
    if (grade == 'A' || grade == 'B' || grade == 'C' || grade == 'D'
       || grade == 'F' || Character.toUpperCase(grade) == 'X') break;
    System.out.println("" + grade + " is an invalid grade. Try again...");
} // while
```

Let's study the above code, because it not only demonstrates a validation loop, but it has a new code variation. The most important thing is that the variable **grade** be declared *above* the validation loop. Otherwise it would not be useable below the loop! It is a rule in Java that variables declared inside a curly-brace container are useable inside that container *only*. If you align your curly-braces correctly, and indent the statements inside as explained in this book, the rule is that a declared variable is no longer useable after the first closing curly-brace *to its left*. This is what's referred to as *scope*.

```
The Scope Of A Variable
{
  ...
  int a;
  ..."a" is useable here...
}
...but not here
```

So the solution is to declare the variable whose value is being input and verified *above* the validation loop.

The validation if-break statement is very lengthy because it has so many tests in it. It's okay to have very long lines in most computer languages, but it makes it hard to read. You could use line wrap in your text editor to see long lines, but it does not follow the indenting rules. So the solution is to split long statements onto separate lines. To split a line, simply place the edit cursor at the position where you want to make the split, and press ENTER. But do not split in the middle of a word or inside quoted text! Now you see why we have the semicolon – *it* marks the end of a statement, and the end of the line does not.

When splitting a statement to two or more lines, it is good practice to indent the second and succeeding lines. In the above example, the normal indent of 2 spaces is used, just as it is with indenting inside curly-brace containers or after single-statement if-statements.

As an alternative, the long if-break could have been separated into multiple if-breaks, like this:

```
if (grade == 'A' || grade == 'B') break;
if (grade == 'C' || grade == 'D') break;
if (grade == 'F' || grade == 'X' || grade == 'x') break;
```

Here's another example of a validation loop:

```
Another Validation Loop

String answer;
while (true)
{
    System.out.print("Your answer [yes/no]: ");
    answer = cin.readLine();
    if (answer.equals("")) continue;
    if (answer.equals("yes")) break;
    if (answer.equals("no")) break;
    System.out.println("Let's try this again...");
} // while
... // resume here after "break"
```

Note the `continue;` statement introduced above. This causes the loop to end the current cycle at that point and go automatically to the next cycle, thus avoiding the "Let's try this again..." prompt if a user just pressed ENTER without typing anything else. There's really no good reason for doing so, other than the opportunity this presents to show how `continue;` works.

6.8 Classic Computer Science Solutions That Use Logic

Two classic problems are finding the lowest (or highest) from among a set of values, and sorting a set of value from lowest to highest (or the reverse). The solutions involve if-statements. They also involve techniques that will be covered in chapters 8 and 11, so while we cannot develop full solutions here, we can at least show the logical parts of the solutions.

6.8.1 Classic Min/Max Logic

A classic problem in computer science is finding the minimum and/or maximum values from among multiple values. For example, given a set of test scores, what are the highest and lowest scores? We still need to get through chapter 11 before we can fully deal with this problem. But now that we can apply logic in our programming, we can at least get a start on the solution. Here are some code blocks to show how this is done:

Finding The Maximum Or Minimum Value

```
// get values for 3 whole numbers
int a = ...
int b = ...
int c = ...

// find the maximum whole number
int max = a;
if (max < b) max = b;
if (max < c) max = c;

// find the minimum whole number
int min = a;
if (min > b) min = b;
if (min > c) min = c;
```

You may not have come up with this logic on your own right away, because it is somewhat counter-intuitive. For example, note that there are variables for storing the minimum and maximum values, but they are set to the value of *the first number*! It's as if we know the answer in advance, and the answer is the first number – we'd have to be pretty lucky for this to work every time!

But the situation is that our if-statements can only compare 2 values at a time, and we have 3. So here's the approach: without looking at any of the numbers, *assume* that the first number is what we want. Then look at the second number, and if it is better, *we change our mind!* Then look at the third number, and if *it* is better, we change our mind, perhaps again. Get used to the idea, because that's a very common approach in programming – assume the answer, then look at alternatives and change your mind when necessary.

You can probably figure out how to extend this to 4 or more values – just add more if-statements.

6.8.2 Classic Sorting Logic
Another classic problem in computer science is reordering multiple values from lowest to highest (or the reverse). We need to get through chapter 11 before we can fully deal with this problem, but we can start here.

```
                   Sorting Values Lo-to-Hi
    // get values for 3 whole numbers
    int a = ...
    int b = ...
    int c = ...

    // move the lowest value to "a"
    if (a > b)
    {
       int temp = a;
       a = b;
       b = temp;
    }
    if (a > c)
    {
       int temp = a;
       a = c;
       c = temp;
    }

    // move the next lowest value to "b"
    if (b > c)
    {
       int temp = b;
       b = c;
       c = temp;
    }

    // ...the highest value is now in "c"
```

Wow – there's a lot of code here! But most of it is repetitious, and will get consolidated as we revisit this in future chapters. The sets of three lines of code, starting with declaration of **temp**, is called "swap code" – it swaps the values of 2 variables in three steps.

As you probably already figured out, this can be adapted to variables of other data types. Just make sure that **temp**'s data type matches that of the others.

6.9 Exercises, Sample Code, Videos, And Addendums

Go to www.rdb3.com/java/6 for extended materials pertaining to this chapter

Chapter 7. More Than One Way: Advanced Branching/Looping

In part 1 of this book we learned to write Java statements to be processed in sequential order, top to bottom. Then in the previous chapter, we learned how statements and code blocks could be skipped over (using if-statements) or repeated (using while-true loops). In this chapter we'll learn other ways to implement branching and looping besides if-statements, if-else, while-true, and if-break. They don't really *add* anything to what we can already do, but they offer us *more concise ways* to write code under certain conditions.

7.1 Multiple Choice If-Statements

Adding `else` after an if-statement, as explained in the previous chapter, simplifies writing code for "true-false" comparisons. The same could be accomplished with *two* separate if-statements, but it's much easier using *one* if-statement with an `else`.

True-False Logic WITHOUT Else

```
if (grade == 'A' || grade == 'B' || grade == 'C')
    System.out.println("You pass");
if (grade != 'A' && grade != 'B' && grade != 'C')
    System.out.println("You do not pass");
```

True-False Logic WITH Else – Much Easier!

```
if (grade == 'A' || grade == 'B' || grade == 'C')
    System.out.println("You pass");
else
    System.out.println("You do not pass");
```

Similarly, it's even more complicated to program "multiple choice" comparisons using lots of separate if-statements, so the Java language does offer another, more direct way, called `else if`.

Using "else-if" logic, if-statements can have zero, one, two, or more **else if**s to test for multiple choices. Once an **if** or **else if** is found to be true, no further checking of any remaining **else if**s happens. There can be a **else** at the end, or not, but it *must* come after any **else if**s. Each **else if** has its own indented statement or curly-brace contained code block(s).

Here's an example:

the algorithm for else-if logic:
get user's grade via keyboard
if A, output "excellent"
otherwise if B, output "good"
otherwise if C, output "average"
otherwise if D or F, output "see ya..."
otherwise, output "invalid"

Using Else-If Logic [Grades.java]

```java
import java.io.*;

public class Grades
{
    public static void main(String[] argv) throws Exception
    {
        BufferedReader cin;
        cin = new BufferedReader(new InputStreamReader(System.in));

        char grade;
        System.out.print("What is your grade? [A, B, C, D, or F]: ");
        grade = cin.readLine().charAt(0);

        if (grade == 'A')
            System.out.println("Excellent");
        else if (grade == 'B')
            System.out.println("Good");
        else if (grade == 'C')
            System.out.println("Average");
        else if (grade == 'D' || grade == 'F')
            System.out.println("See you next year");
        else
            System.out.println("Invalid: " + grade);
    }
}
```

Another example shows how to compare two numbers, in order to find which is greater – or if they are the same. It uses else-if logic, and the **else** is reached when neither number is greater than the other – that is, they are the same. There's no need to check with ▆▆ because there's nothing else it could be!

the algorithm for comparing two numbers:
read the 1st number from the keyboard
read the 2nd number from the keyboard
if the 1st number is smaller than the 2nd
    output that it is so
otherwise if the 2nd number is smaller than the 1st
    output that it is so
otherwise
    output that the numbers are the same

Comparing Numbers With Else-If [Compare2Numbers.java]

```java
import java.io.*;

public class Compare2Numbers
{
  public static void main(String[] argv) throws Exception
  {
    BufferedReader cin;
    cin = new BufferedReader(new InputStreamReader(System.in));

    int a;
    System.out.print("Enter the 1st number: ");
    a = new Double(cin.readLine()).intValue();

    int b;
    System.out.print("Enter the 2nd number: ");
    b = new Double(cin.readLine()).intValue();

    if (a < b)
        System.out.println("" + a + " is less than " + b);
    else if (b < a)
        System.out.println("" + b + " is less than " + a);
    else
        System.out.println("" + a + " is the same as " + b);
  }
}
```

7.1.1 Alternate Code For Multiple Choice Comparisons

A drawback of the else-if logic in the **Grades.java** program shown above is the requirement to repeat the tested variable over and over again. The Java language provides another way to represent the same logic without such repetition – the "switch-statement". Here's an example:

Using A Switch-Statement [`GradeSwitch.java`]

```java
import java.io.*;

public class GradeSwitch
{
  public static void main(String[] argv) throws Exception
  {
    BufferedReader cin;
    cin = new BufferedReader(new InputStreamReader(System.in));

    char grade;
    System.out.print("What is your grade? [A, B, C, D, or F]: ");
    grade = cin.readLine().charAt(0);

    switch (grade)
    {                                              // start here with switch OFF
      case 'A':                                    // if grade is 'A', turn switch ON
      case 'a':                                    // if grade is 'a', turn switch ON
        System.out.println("Excellent");           // do this if switch is ON
        break;                                     // skip to closing curly-brace if switch is ON
      case 'B':                                    // if grade is 'B', turn switch ON
      case 'b':                                    // if grade is 'b', turn switch ON
        System.out.println("Good");                // do this if switch is ON
        break;                                     // skip to closing curly-brace if switch is ON
      case 'C':                                    // if grade is 'C', turn switch ON
      case 'c':                                    // if grade is 'c', turn switch ON
        System.out.println("Average");             // do this if switch is ON
        break;                                     // skip to closing curly-brace if switch is ON
      case 'D':                                    // if grade is 'D', turn switch ON
      case 'F':                                    // if grade is 'F', turn switch ON
      case 'd':                                    // if grade is 'd', turn switch ON
      case 'f':                                    // if grade is 'f', turn switch ON
        System.out.println("See you next year");   // do this if switch is ON
        break;                                     // skip to closing curly-brace if switch is ON
      default:                                     // turn switch ON
        System.out.println("Invalid: " + grade);   // do this if switch is ON
    }                                              // this is the closing curly-brace
  }
}
```

The keyword **switch** can be used to test whole numbers or single-character text only – *not* floating point numbers or any-size text. The **break;** statement marks the end of a code block. Curly-braces are not required for the code blocks that belong to cases, even if they have more than one statement! *But* if there are any declaration statements, then a curly-brace container *is* needed. The **default:** condition works like the **else** with if-statements – it is not required, and does not need to end in **break;**.

When using **switch** with whole numbers, use statements like **case 0:**, without quote marks around the tested value. But when using **switch** with single-character text, use statements like **case 'A':**, *with* single quote marks around the tested value.

Switch-statements cannot have ranges or variables in their `case` statements.

The switch-statement gets its name from the fact that it is like an on/off switch. It starts in the "off" position, and checks each `case` statement from top to bottom until it finds a match with the value in its parentheses. When (and if) a match is found, or if the `default` statement is reached, the switch is set to "on". From then on, all other `case` statements are ignored, and any code that appears is executed. The purpose of `break;` is to prevent sequential processing from going any further, and running into and over the next `case` – it skips to the end of the switch-statement, after its closing curly-brace.

But *beware the switch-statement!* Do not use `switch` in place of if-break logic. The reason is that the `break;` statement inside a `switch` means something entirely different than what it means in an if-break. It exits the `switch`, and has no effect on any loop that may contain it.

7.2 Event-Controlled vs Count-Controlled Loops

There are two basic loop types: "event-controlled" and "count-controlled". The difference is a conceptual one, having to do with knowing *in advance* the number of cycles the loop will execute. In event-controlled loops, cycles continue until certain conditions are met that allow an if-break to exit the loop. When such conditions are met, that's an "event". The number of cycles that will be executed before the event occurs cannot be determined ahead of time. Every loop example in the previous chapter was event-controlled.

The types of event that can cause the end of an event-controlled loop include (1) user enters "quit" in response to a prompt, (2) a valid input value is entered, (3) the end of a file is reached while reading a file, as we'll study in chapter 10, or (4) satisfying any other logical condition that should make the loop end.

By contrast, a count-controlled loop executes a *predetermined* number of cycles. So a loop that outputs your name repeatedly until the user tells it to stop is *event-controlled*. And a loop to output your name exactly 10 times is *count-controlled*.

If the number of cycles of a loop is known ahead of time, use a *count-controlled loop*. It's similar to an event-controlled loop, but the "event" is reaching the predetermined number of cycles. Count-controlled loops use an **int** to keep track of the number of cycles, and it is the value of this "counter" that is compared in an "if-break".

A Count-Controlled Loop

```
int i; // cycle counter
i = 0; // zero cycles so far
while (true)
{
    if (i == 10) break; // do 10 cycles
    . . .
    i = i + 1;
}
```

The counter in count-controlled loops is traditionally declared as **i**. The last statement in the loop "increments" **i** – that is, it adds one to it. But the logic to control this loop is all over the place – before the loops starts, at the top of the loop's curly-brace container, and at the bottom of the container. A purpose of this chapter is to introduce other ways to do such loops in more concise ways.

Actually the counter can be incremented anywhere else in the loop, and it can still work the same. But it's better to perform the incrementing at the *end* of the loop for reasons that will become clearer as we go forward.

7.2.1 The While-Condition Loop

In the next example, the previous count-controlled loop is simplified a little bit by putting something other than **true** inside the **while**'s parentheses:

```
              A While-Condition Loop
int i; // cycle counter
i = 0; // zero cycles so far
while (i != 10) // do exactly 10 cycles
{
   . . .
  i = i + 1;
}
```

The while-condition statement combines the while-true and if-break into *one* statement. Instead of breaking when the counter reaches 10, we continue the loop as long as the counter is *not* 10. The expression inside the if-break's parentheses got moved into the `while`'s parentheses, but its logic had to be *reversed*! Break if equal, keep going while *not* equal.

While-condition can be used for both event-controlled and count-controlled loops. Remember – count-controlled loops are really just event-controlled loops where the "event" is the counter reaching its limit.

Here's the rule for when you can use while-condition instead of while-true-if-break: if there's an if-break statement as the *first statement* inside the loop's curly-brace container, you can use while-condition instead. You don't have to, but you can.

Here is a full example of a *count-controlled loop* using while-condition. It tracks the height that a dropped ball bounces, by cutting the height by 50% with each successive bounce. It tracks this for exactly 10 bounces, starting from a height of 40 (inches).

A Simple Count-Controlled Loop [Bounce.java]

```
public class Bounce
{
  public static void main(String[] argv)
  {
    double height = 40;

    int i;
    i = 0;
    while (i < 10)
    {
      height = height / 2;
      System.out.println("location is now: " + height + " inches");
      i = i + 1;
    } // while
  } // main
} // public class
```

The last statement in this count-controlled loop *increments* the counter, **i**. Since incrementing **int**'s is done so often in programming, Java has a shorthand way to write $i = i + 1;$ – it's $i++;$. The statement $i = i + 1;$ actually consists of two steps: addition and assignment. So it seems useful to have a statement that does both in one operation. And yes, there's a $i--;$ too, that subtracts 1 from **i**. But whatever you do, don't ever write ~~$i = i++;$~~ or anything like that – results are unpredictable.

7.2.2 The Do-While Loop

In a while-condition, the if-break at the *top* of the curly-brace container got merged with the **while**. But what if there's an if-break at the bottom of the container, as in 6.7.3's **ThereYet.java**? In that case you can use a "do-while" instead:

Using Do-While [`ThereYet2.java`]

```java
import java.io.*;

public class ThereYet2
{
  public static void main(String[] argv) throws Exception
  {
    BufferedReader cin;
    cin = new BufferedReader(new InputStreamReader(System.in));

    String answer;
    do
    {
      System.out.print("Are we there yet? ");
      answer = cin.readLine();
    } while (!answer.equals("yes"));
  } // main
} // public class
```

Again, note the reverse logic – break if the answer's "yes", keep going while the answer's *not* "yes". The do-while variation usually applies to event-controlled loop logic.

7.3 Introducing The For-Loop

Count-controlled loops have three control steps that are each done separately but are all required in order for the loop to work right. So like most languages, Java provides a variation called the "for-loop", which combines all three into one statement. Here's an adaptation of **Bounce.java** from above, using a for-loop:

<u>the algorithm for a simple count-controlled loop:</u>
initialize height to 40
loop starts here
10X divide height by 2
output height to the console
loop ends here

A Simple Count-Controlled Loop [Bounce2.java]

```
public class Bounce2
{
  public static void main(String[] argv)
  {
    double height = 40;

    int i;
    for (i = 0; i != 10; i = i + 1)
    {
      height = height / 2;
      System.out.println("location is now: " + height + " inches");
    } // for
  } // main
} // public class
```

The **for** statement has three distinct parts to it, separated by two semicolons. The first part has the counter's initialization $\boxed{i = 0}$. Later we'll put its declaration there, too.

The middle part has a reverse-logic version of the if-break – with if-break it's break when the counter reaches its limit (10), and with the for-loop it's keep going while the counter is *not* at its limit. Later we'll see this common variation: keep going while the counter is *less than* its limit.

The last part is the increment statement, $\boxed{i = i + 1}$. Later we'll see this variation: $\boxed{i++}$.

7.3.1 The Traditional For-Loop
The loop in **Bounce2.java** matches the count-controlled while-true-if-break examples that preceded it. But if you had jumped into for-loops without first studying **while**, you probably would have seen them written with the variations referred to above. This is the way you'll usually see for-loops written:

```
for (int i = 0; i < 10; i++)
{
  height = height / 2;
  System.out.println("location is now: " + height + " inches");
} // for
```

The only real difference in these two for-loop variations is that the counter `i` exists only within the loop when it's declared inside the `for` itself.

Most of the examples in this book use the traditional variation, with the counter declared inside the `for`, the *less-than* logic instead of *not equals*, and the `i++` increment statement. Most – but not all.

7.3.2 Variable For-Loop Limits

In the for-loops presented above, the limit is expressed as a number – 10. That is, the loop will run for exactly 10 cycles. But the limit can also be expressed as an `int` *variable*. In the next example, the user specifies via the keyboard how may numbers to send to output, starting with one:

```
                Counting From Zero [CountFromZero.java]

import java.io.*;

public class CountFromZero
{
  public static void main(String[] argv) throws Exception
  {
    BufferedReader cin;
    cin = new BufferedReader(new InputStreamReader(System.in));

    int n; // print this many numbers
    System.out.print("How many numbers to output? ");
    n = new Double(cin.readLine()).intValue();

    int number = 1;
    for (int i = 0; i < n; i++)
    {
      System.out.print(number + " ");
      number++; // becomes next higher number
    } // for
    System.out.println();
  } // main
} // public class
```

output: 1 2 3 4 5 6 ...

7.3.3 Counting Backwards

Unless you know exactly what you are doing, you should always write count-controlled loops so that their counter starts from zero and moves forward. When writing a loop that is supposed to count backwards, resist the temptation to use such expressions as `i--` in the for-loop. It's not that it won't work, because it does work. It's just difficult for beginners to make it work *properly*.

Instead, setup the count control as has been suggested and demonstrated in this chapter, and use *another* variable for the backwards-travelling value. Initialize that variable, and subtract from it in the count-controlled loop. In this way you separate the processes of managing the cycles of the loop, and counting backwards. Actually, **Bounce.java** from section 7.2.1 suggests how this might be done.

Here's an example that sends a numeric sequence of 16 numbers to output, *backwards* from 99:

Backwards For-Loop [Backwards.java]

```java
public class Backwards
{
  public static void main(String[] argv)
  {
    int number = 99;
    for (int i = 0; i < 16; i++)
    {
      System.out.print(number + " ");
      number--; // becomes next lower number
    } // for
    System.out.println();
  } // main
} // public class
```

output: 99 98 97 96 95 94 93 92 91 90 89 88 87 86 85 84

7.3.4 Classic Min/Max Loop

As it was presented in the previous chapter, a classic min/max problem is finding the largest and smallest among three values. In this variation we find the largest and smallest among an *unlimited* number of values, using an event-controlled loop. The loop is controlled using the "sentinel method" – when the user enters a certain value outside of the expected range of values, it is a signal to exit the loop. As in the example from the previous chapter, we use test scores whose values are expected to be in the range of 0 to 100. Here are some code blocks that show how this is done:

Finding The Maximum Or Minimum Value Using Loops

```
// find the maximum score
int sentinel = -999; // an unexpected score value
int max = sentinel; // signifies that max is not yet set
while (true)
{
  int aScore;
  System.out.print("Enter a score [" + sentinel + " to exit]: ");
  aScore = new Double(cin.readLine()).intValue();
  if (aScore == sentinel) break; // that's the signal to exit this loop
  if (max == sentinel || max < aScore) max = aScore;
}

// find the minimum score
int sentinel = -999; // an unexpected score value
int min = sentinel; // signifies that min is not yet set
while (true)
{
  int aScore;
  System.out.print("Enter a score [" + sentinel + " to exit]: ");
  aScore = new Double(cin.readLine()).intValue();

  if (aScore == sentinel) break; // that's the signal to exit this loop
  if (min == sentinel || min > aScore) min = aScore;
}

// find the max AND min scores
int sentinel = -999; // an unexpected score value
int max = sentinel; // signifies that max is not yet set
int min = sentinel; // signifies that min is not yet set
while (true)
{
  int aScore;
  System.out.print("Enter a score [" + sentinel + " to exit]: ");
  aScore = new Double(cin.readLine()).intValue();
  if (aScore == sentinel) break; // that's the signal to exit this loop
  if (max == sentinel || max < aScore) max = aScore;
  if (min == sentinel || min > aScore) min = aScore;
}
```

The `if (aScore == sentinel) break;` statement
is easy to understand – it exits the loop if the sentinel value gets
entered. But what about `if (max == sentinel ...` ?
That's there so that the maximum and/or minimum get set to the
first-entered value no matter what it is. Remember that the first-
entered value will necessarily be the maximum *and* the minimum
until something else comes along to replace it.

Try this modification: you can avoid the issue of a sentinel if you
first prompt the user for the number of scores to be entered. But
you still have to figure out how to initialize **max** and **min**. An
old trick is to initialize **max** to a very large negative number, so
that no matter what the first entry is, it will be larger. Likewise,

initialize **min** to a very large positive number, so that no matter what the first entry is, it will be smaller.

Here is another feature of the above code blocks that you should notice and learn by the example it provides. Note that **sentinel** is created to store **-999**, and note that the value **-999** therefore only has to appear once. It is good programming practice to write a value only once, so that if you change it, you only have to do so in one place. You'll see that this requires the "Enter a score" prompt to be a bit more complicated than usual, to include **sentinel**.

7.4 Nested Loops

"Nesting" is when there is a loop *inside* the curly-brace container of another loop. In each cycle of the outer-most loop, *all* cycles of the innermost loop are run. The concept of nesting is not just for for-loops – it's for loops in general, both count-controlled and event-controlled. But the examples that follow are all nested for-loops. Nested count-controlled loops need *two* loop counters – one to remember how many times we've been through the "outer loop" while another counts the cycles of the "inner loop".

A classic programming puzzle is to use nested loops to create two-dimensional patterns in rows and columns of the output. For example, here is a program that reads a number for the keyboard, and outputs that many rows of stars. The first row contains one star, and each succeeding row contains one additional star. Note that this uses a variable **n** for the cycle limit.

Right-Triangle Pattern [`RightTriangle.java`]

```java
import java.io.*;

public class RightTriangle
{
  public static void main(String[] argv) throws Exception
  {
    BufferedReader cin;
    cin = new BufferedReader(new InputStreamReader(System.in));

    int n; // print this many rows
    System.out.print("How many rows to print? ");
    n = new Double(cin.readLine()).intValue();

    for (int i = 0; i < n; i++)
    {
      for (int j = 0; j < (i + 1); j++)
        System.out.print('*');
      System.out.println();
    } // for
  } // main
} // public class
```

Look at the j-loop. It cycles `i + 1` times. Since `i` is zero the first time through, `i + 1` is one, and the j-loop causes 1 star to be sent to output before the **println** skips to the next line. The next time through, `i` is one, and `i + 1` is two, so the j-loop causes 2 stars to be sent to output before **println**, and so on.

In the following, a pyramid shape is drawn with two additional stars in each succeeding row – one added to the left and one to the right of the preceding row. The challenge here is to put spaces in front of all rows except the last.

Pyramid Pattern [Pyramid.java]

```java
import java.io.*;

public class Pyramid
{
    public static void main(String[] argv) throws Exception
    {
        BufferedReader cin;
        cin = new BufferedReader(new InputStreamReader(System.in));

        int n; // print this many rows
        System.out.print("How many rows to print? ");
        n = new Double(cin.readLine()).intValue();

        int stars = 1;
        int skip = n - 1;
        for (int i = 0; i < n; i++)
        {
            int j;
            for (j = 0; j < skip; j++) System.out.print(' ');
            for (j = 0; j < stars; j++) System.out.print('*');
            System.out.println();
            stars += 2;
            --skip;
        } // for
    } // main
} // public class
```

Note that there are two additional variables for tracking how many stars to show in each row, and how many spaces to skip before writing the stars. They are separate from the loop counters. Let loop counters be loop counters – if you need something else, declare and manage another variable for whatever that purpose may be.

In any case, the first row has only one star, and each additional row has two more stars than the last – that's why the statement `stars += 2;` is there. The number of spaces in front of the first row's star is `n - 1` – you would have to write a star-containing pyramid on paper to figure out this number. The number of skips decreases by one with each successive row, hence the `skip--;`.

Finally, note that `j` is declared above the two loops that use it. If you have two loops – one after the other – and you want to reuse the first's counter variable in the second loop, do it this way. Also note that the loops are one-liners, and that is a form of a loop that is described in the section 7.6.3 below.

Here is another modification – it reflects the pyramid around its last row to form a diamond shape. All rows except the last are repeated in reverse order.

```
                    Diamond Pattern [Diamond.java]

import java.io.*;

public class Diamond
{
    public static void main(String[] argv) throws Exception
    {
        BufferedReader cin;
        cin = new BufferedReader(new InputStreamReader(System.in));

        int n; // print this many rows
        System.out.print("How many rows to print? ");
        n = new Double(cin.readLine()).intValue();

        int stars = 1;
        int skip = n - 1;
        int i;
        for (i = 0; i < n; i++)
        {
            int j;
            for (j = 0; j < skip; j++) System.out.print(' ');
            for (j = 0; j < stars; j++) System.out.print('*');
            System.out.println();
            stars += 2;
            --skip;
        } // for

        stars = 2 * n - 3;
        skip = 1;
        int extraRows = n - 1;
        for (i = 0; i < extraRows; i++)
        {
            int j;
            for (j = 0; j < skip; j++) System.out.print(' ');
            for (j = 0; j < stars; j++) System.out.print('*');
            System.out.println();
            stars -= 2;
            ++skip;
        } // for
    } // main
} // public class
```

Note that the two variables for tracking the number of stars and skips are reset so that the first line of the reflection will come out right. Then the i-loop is modified to cycle one less time, because the last row is not repeated. Then the number of stars *decreases* by 2 and the number of spaces increases by 1 with each reflected row.

Finally, note that **i** is declared separately, because there are two i-loops. Try these, to see the patterns they make! Change the logic to design your own patters, so that you gain a better understanding of how nested loops work.

7.4.1 A Digital Clock Simulation

This example not only shows *multiple* levels of nesting, but it also demonstrates a few new programming techniques: "sleep" which is useful in computer "simulations" and game programming, the "carriage return" which can be used to overwrite previously displayed output, and animated output formatting.

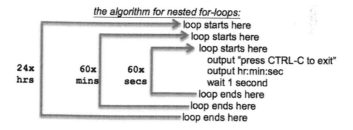

the algorithm for nested for-loops:

More Nested For-Loops [`DigitalClock.java`]

```java
import java.text.*;

public class DigitalClock
{
  public static void main(String[] argv) throws Exception
  {
    System.out.println("CTRL-C to exit...");
    for (int hr = 0; hr < 24; hr++)
    {
      for (int min = 0; min < 60; min++)
      {
        for (int sec = 0; sec < 60; sec++)
        {
          System.out.print("" + new DecimalFormat("00").format(hr));
          System.out.print(":" + new DecimalFormat("00").format(min));
          System.out.print(":" + new DecimalFormat("00").format(sec) + ' ');
          System.out.flush();
          Thread.sleep(1000); // one second
          System.out.print('\r'); // carriage return
        }
      }
    }
  } // main
} // public class
```

This example has *three* levels of nesting, requiring *three* counters. It also demonstrates another way to name counters that is more descriptive than `i` and `j`. The outer loop counts hours, so its counter is named `hr`. The innermost loop counts seconds, so its counter is named `sec`. The middle loop counts minutes, so its counter is named `min`. Name counters as you wish, as long as their names follow variable naming rules as explained in chapter 3.

"Sleep" is when a program pauses for a predetermined amount of time, usually measured in milliseconds. `throws Exception` is appended to `public static void main` because of the statement `Thread.sleep(1000);`, which requires it.

A carriage return is an old, typewriter term for moving back to the beginning of a line. Sending `'\r'` to output before `print` gives us a way to overwrite the last output *without* scrolling to the next line. The visual effect is that the part of the display being overwritten appears to be animated.

`System.out.flush()` is not necessary on every system, but it's a good idea to have it so that your program works on all systems. Some systems do not show on the console screen everything that is sent to output right away – they "buffer" it and send it when the buffer is full, or a line feed is sent. Flushing the buffer causes the output to appear even if the buffer is not full.

7.5 Four Forms Of The If-Statement

Several different forms of the if-statement have been presented so far, including with and without curly-brace containers. This section summarizes the four different ways that you can write such statements:

7.5.1 `if` With A Curly-Brace Container

The most common example has a multi-statement code block inside a curly-brace container. When the condition in the parentheses of the if-statement evaluates to *true*, the container's code is *not* skipped.

If-Statement With Curly-Brace Container
| ```
if (...)
{
    ...
    ...        one or more
    ...        statements
    ...
}
``` |

Actually, this form can be used even when there is only one statement in the container. Some programmers prefer to always use a container, even if there's just one statement in it.

7.5.2 `if` Without A Curly-Brace Container

Another common example has a single-statement code block without curly-braces. When the condition in the parentheses of the if-statement evaluates to *true*, the statement is *not* skipped.
```

If-Statement Without Curly-Brace Container
```
if (...)
    statement;
```

This offers a more condensed way to write code, without doubling the amount of vertical space by including curly-braces.

7.5.3 `if` All On One Line
A single-statement code block can also follow the `if` on the same line, condensing the code even further.

One-Line If-Statement
```
if (...) statement;
```

This is suitable for very short, single statements.

7.5.4 Beware! `if` With Semicolon
There is no good reason to use this form, but it is valid, and your program will compile if you use it. The semicolon after the condition's parentheses effectively cuts off the if-statement from whatever follows it – indented or not!

If-Statement With Semicolon
```
if (...);
```

The only reason for showing this form is to make you aware of this pitfall. It is a difficult programming error to diagnose, because the compiler accepts it and it leads to logically incorrect results when the program runs. It's not uncommon for beginners to fall into this trap:

An If-Statement That DOES NOT WORK AS EXPECTED!!!
```
if (grade == 'A');
    System.out.println("excellent");
```

This sends "excellent" to the console screen for *any* value of `grade` – not just `'A'`. The reason is that the semicolon at the end of the if-statement *ends* the statement! Even though it is indented, the output statement does *not* belong to the `if`. It is a separate statement, as if it was not indented at all.

But it does compile, and that is the unfortunate part – compilers allow you to do this even though you probably would prefer that it gave a compilation error. There is one exception – if you add an `else` or `else if`, it will be seen as standing alone without an `if`, and compilers won't allow that!

7.6 Four Forms Of Loops

Several examples of loops have been presented so far, nearly all written with curly-brace containers, but some as one-liners. Similar to the if-statement, loops whose code block consists of only one statement do not need curly-brace containers. This section summarizes the four different ways that you can write loops, and although this applies to all kinds, `while` and `for` loops are used to demonstrate:

7.6.1 Loop With A Curly-Brace Container
The most common example has a multi-statement code block contained in curly-braces. Presumably there are one or more if-break statements in the code block.

```
Loop With A Curly-Brace Container
  while (true)
  {
     . . .
     . . .      one or more
     . . .      statements
     . . .
  }
```

Actually, this form can be used even when there is only one statement in the code block.

7.6.2 Loop Without A Curly-Brace Container
Another common example has a single-statement code block without curly-braces. While the condition in the parentheses of the

loop statement (between the 2 semicolons) evaluates to true, its statement is repeated.

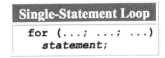

```
Single-Statement Loop
    for (...; ...; ...)
        statement;
```

This offers a more condensed way to write code, without doubling the amount of vertical space by including curly-braces.

7.6.3 Loop All On One Line
A single-statement code block can also follow the **for** on the same line, condensing the code even further.

```
          One-Line Loop
    for (...; ...; ...) statement;
```

7.6.4 Beware! A Loop With A Semicolon
You may see no good reason to use this form, but there is, and you will see it in part 3 of this book. The semicolon after the **while**'s or **for**'s parentheses effectively cuts off the **while** or **for** statement from whatever follows it – indented or not!

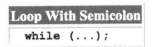

```
Loop With Semicolon
    while (...);
```

It's not uncommon for beginners to do this:

```
A Loop Statement That DOES NOT WORK AS EXPECTED!!!
    for (int i = 0; i < 10; i++);
        System.out.println("Hello!");
```

This sends "Hello!" to output *once*. The reason is that the semicolon at the end of the **for** *ends* the loop! Even though it is indented, the output statement does *not* belong to the loop. It is a separate statement, as if it was not indented at all. That's true even if a curly-brace container is used.

7.7 Advanced Logic Considerations

You'd think that comparison operators and and-logic and or-logic would be all you need for branching and looping, and you're right – *mostly*! There are a couple of situations that arise frequently, that require a bit of thought to figure out. So here are some programming "tricks" to help you deal with them

7.7.1 Comparing Any-Length Text
Remember **CrossTheRoad.java** in section 6.7.3, where we figured out a way to allow "yes" to be entered as an uppercase "Y" or a lowercase "y"? First we were surprised to find that it even made a difference! Y is Y, right? Well, not necessarily. *Case matters* in programming. "Y" is not "y", and it makes a difference when using them in comparison statements.

We solved that problem in **CrossTheRoad.java**, but we totally ignored it in the **ThereYet.java** program that preceded it. That's because **ThereYet.java** used an any-length `String` variable instead of a `char`, complicating the matter. So rather than recognize and deal with it, we ignored it. We can ignore it no longer.

In the following example, only the answer "Red" gets checked – that uppercase "R" and lowercase "e" and "d". It's the only version of the word's "casing" that we check.

Testing Input Text [RedGreen.java]

```java
import java.io.*;

public class RedGreen
{
  public static void main(String[] argv) throws Exception
  {
    BufferedReader cin;
    cin = new BufferedReader(new InputStreamReader(System.in));

    String light;
    System.out.print("What color is the light? [Red/Green]: ");
    light = cin.readLine();

    if (light.equals("Red"))
      System.out.println("Stop and wait");
  }
}
```

But what if the user types "red" instead of "Red"? What if the user types "rEd"? In those situations the user will not be warned to stop and wait! This is the issue of "case" – uppercase, lowercase, and "mixed case". We could do `if (light == "red" || light == "Red" || light == "rEd")`, but there are too many combinations for this approach to be practical.

The solution is to read the keyboard input, copy it, and convert the copy to lowercase. Then test the lowercase copy.

the algorithm for testing input text:
ask user to enter color, red or green
create a copy of the user's answer
convert the copy to lowercase
if the converted lowercase copy is "red"
  output "stop"

Testing Input Text [RedGreen2.java]

```java
import java.io.*;

public class RedGreen2
{
    public static void main(String[] argv) throws Exception
    {
        BufferedReader cin;
        cin = new BufferedReader(new InputStreamReader(System.in));

        String light;
        System.out.print("What color is the light? [Red/Green]: ");
        light = cin.readLine();

        String lcLight = light.toLowerCase(); // a copy of light

        if (lcLight.equals("red"))
            System.out.println("Stop and wait");
    }
}
```

The statement

```java
String lcLight = light.toLowerCase();
```

creates a lowercase copy of the String `light`.

Then the "if" statement needs only to test against the lowercase version of the answer, "red".

Another way this could have been done in Java would be to use the statement `if (light.equalsIgnoreCase("red"))` instead. This would make a case independent comparison, and the conversion statement would not have been needed.

7.7.2 Reverse Logic

Logical expressions evaluate to true or false. Sometimes when formulating a logical expression for a programming solution, the logic ends up being the opposite of what was intended. For example, you might come up with "if this condition happens, skip the next code block" when what you really wanted is "if this condition happens, *execute* the next code block". So you would have to reverse the "if" logic. Or you may find it necessary to rewrite a code block in such a way that the originally written logical expression needs to be reformulated as its opposite. For example, the original code block might output "password accepted", but we want to change it to say "invalid password – try again".

There are several different ways to reverse a logical expression, and three of them are presented here. The one you choose depends on the form of the original logical expression.

Using Opposite Operators. If the original expression is a simple comparison with one comparison operator, swap out the operator with its opposite. Swap `==` with `!=`, `<` with `>=`, or `>` with `<=`, and vice versa.

Using "Not" Logic. No matter what the original expression is, you can always enclose it in parentheses and put a "not-operator" in front. The not-operator is an exclamation point. So the logical opposite of `if (grade == 'A')` is `if (!(grade == 'A'))`. The logical opposite of `if (grade == 'A' || grade == 'B' || grade == 'C')` is `if (!(grade == 'A' || grade == 'B' || grade == 'C'))`. This uses "nested parentheses" – parentheses inside another set of parentheses. That's perfectly okay in programming, just try to keep them "balanced" – that is, make sure each opening parenthesis has a matching closing one.

Using DeMorgan's Theorem. DeMorgan's Theorem can be applied to expressions that have and-logic or or-logic in them. It is done by swapping `==` with `!=`, `<` with `>=`, or `>` with `<=` (and vise versa), where they appear. Then swap `&&` with `||` (and vise versa). For example, the reverse of `answer == 'y' || answer == 'Y'` is `answer != 'y' && answer != 'Y'`. Remember the "True-false Logic WITHOUT Else" code sample from section 7.1? That actually used DeMorgan's Theorem in the second `if`, to get the opposite of the first `if`.

7.7.3 Scope Issues In Curly-Brace Containers

The possibility of curly-brace containers *inside* other curly-brace containers raises an interesting question: can you declare variables of the same name in each set of curly-braces, like this?

```
                    A Scope Issue
int x; // first declaration
...
{
    ...
    int x; // second declaration
    ...
}
```

In Java, the first declaration is okay. But the second one causes a compiler error, since it is seen as an attempt to redeclare a variable.

7.8 Exercises, Sample Code, Videos, And Addendums

Go to www.rdb3.com/java/7 for extended materials pertaining to this chapter.

Chapter 8. Simplifying Complicated Programs: Using Functions

Java's subprograms are called "functions". What you need to know about functions is why they are used in programming, the distinction between "void functions" and "value-returning functions", and how "parameter lists" work. You also need to know about two kinds of functions – the ones in the compiler's library, and the ones written by you, the programmer. For library functions you need to know the correct `import` to use in order to have access to any particular function. Note that many of the more common Java library functions do not need `import`. For ones you write, you need to know what are "function definitions" and "function calls", and how to use them.

Things started to get a bit complicated when we introduced validation loops. What used to be a simple set of a few lines of code grew into nearly a dozen lines, with a loop and indented statements inside a curly-brace container. All we wanted to do was transfer one value from the keyboard. It would have been nice to say in one statement: "get a valid value for grade from the keyboard", but it took ten times as many statements with prompts and a loop.

Programs don't have to get too much more complicated than they already are before the code listings get so bogged down in detail that it gets hard to follow the logic. Imagine **ItsAboutYou.java** from chapter 5, if we were to add validation to each of its 4 console keyboard inputs – and that program does not even process the inputs or produce any output!

To accommodate this situation, programming languages provide ways to *modularize* code by using "subprograms", or what we're calling "functions" in Java. Remember `Math.pow(1 + p, T)` from chapter 4's **AmortizationCalc.java**? That uses a function to remove the details of raising a number to a power from the main sequential processing flow. Raising a number to a power is so commonly used that the computer language's compiler already has the function in its library, ready for you to use.

But there are not functions in the compiler's library to do all the things we would ever want to do. Certainly there are none to validate our example's grade input. We'll learn in this chapter how to write and use our own functions. We'll use them to modularize our programs by removing detailed code blocks from the main sequential processing flow of a program, placing them into separate functions.

8.1 Value-Returning Functions

Let's start with an input validation example that moves the details of input validation into a function.

Look for these three main parts *inside* the function, because they provide beginning programmers with a formula for success when learning to write their own value-returning functions. You can eventually stray from this exact formulation, as most programmers do, but not until you know *exactly* what you are doing!

3 Parts Of A Value-Returning Function

1. Declare a variable named `result` with a default value.
2. Write code to possibly reassign a different value to `result`, replacing its default value.
3. "Return" `result`.

Input Validation With A Value-Returning Function [PassingGradeFun.java]

```java
import java.io.*;

public class PassingGradeFun
{
  static char getGrade() throws Exception
  {
    char result = 'X'; // the default value

    BufferedReader cin;
    cin = new BufferedReader(new InputStreamReader(System.in));

    while (true)
    {
      System.out.print("What is your grade? [A, B, C, D, F, or X to quit]: ");
      result = cin.readLine().charAt(0);

      if (result == 'A' || result == 'B' || result == 'C') break;
      if (result == 'D' || result == 'F') break;
      if (result == 'X' || result == 'x') break;

      System.out.println("" + result + " is not a valid grade. Try again...");
    } // while

    return result;
  } // getGrade

  public static void main(String[] argv) throws Exception
  {
    char grade;
    while (true)
    {
      grade = getGrade();
      if (grade == 'X' || grade == 'x') break;
      if (grade == 'A' || grade == 'B' || grade == 'C')
        System.out.println("You pass");
    } // while
    System.out.println("Thanks for checking your grades!");
  } // main
} // public class
```

Okay – so it does not *look* less complicated than it did before without functions. But if you look at **main**, you will notice that *it* is simpler. The code for prompting the user and the loop for validating the input are all replaced with one statement, **grade = getGrade();**.

Let's take apart the above example in order to understand how value-returning functions work.

8.1.1 The Function Call
getGrade() is a function call. It is an *expression* that invokes the function, suspending main's sequential processing flow until

124

the function finishes. The call resolves to a value, just as if it was a variable name, and since it is used in an assignment statement, that value gets stored in the variable `grade`.

Function names follow the same rules for identifiers as variables do. So how can the compiler tell that `getGrade` is a function and not a variable? It can tell because functions have parentheses after the identifier and variables do not. While `grade = getGrade();` is a function call, `grade = getGrade;` would expect `getGrade` to represent a variable (which it does not!)

Actually, the same function call can be used in programs more than once, if you have the need to do so. A call can be used anywhere that you would otherwise use a value, variable, or expression – even inside the body of its own "definition" (yikes!) But in our case, we only need it once (whew!)

8.1.2 The Function Definition

After the `import` statement(s) and `public class`, we are used to seeing `public static void main`, but this is not the case in our example. Now, there is another structure, very similar to the one for main, which comes above main. That is the "function definition" – it has a curly-brace container for the detailed code that got removed from main where it was replaced by a call. It gets run whenever a call is made that references it by its name.

The first line of a function definition is the "function header". In our example it's `static char getGrade()`.The "static" keyword is required. (The "public" keyword that appears with main's header is optional except for main, and so it's left out.) A curly-brace container follows the header, with the function's code block(s).

The keyword `char` denotes that the function results in a data value of type `char`. This is called the "return type" of the function. All other data types are valid return types, but there can be only one per function.

`getGrade` is the programmer-selected name of the function. It is to be used in expressions that call the function from "main". The empty parentheses are required, indicating that the identifier "getGrade" refers to a function instead of a variable.

8.1.3 The `return` Statement

A value-returning function should have a `return` statement as the last statement in its definition. Following the keyword "return", there needs to be a value, variable, or expression that matches the return type. In our case, it will usually be `return result;` .

8.1.4 Doing Console Input Or File I/O In A Java Function

Note that the function header includes `throws Exception`. This is because `cin` is used inside that function for keyboard input. It would also be required for `fin` and `fout`, which are used for file I/O. Even though `cin` is not used in "main", it still needs `throws Exception` in *its* header, because it calls a function that has `throws Exception` in *its* header.

8.2 Parameter Lists

Note that the parentheses of `getGrade` are empty in **PassingGradeFun.java**. But the parentheses of **Math.pow** are *not* empty in **AmortizationCalc.java** from chapter 4. A function's parentheses identify it as a function instead of a variable. But they also are a container for *inputs* to the function. It is a way for the call to send values to the function for processing. The function call `Math.pow(1 + p, T)` has two inputs separated by commas. This list of comma-separated inputs is called the "parameter list".

If a function has empty parentheses, then it has no inputs, like `getGrade`. The number and type of the values in the parameter list of a call *must* match what the function expects them to be. This is specified in the "header". So since the header for `getGrade` has empty parentheses, the call must have empty parentheses, too.

In the `Math.pow` calls, the expression `1 + p` is resolved first, by retrieving the value stored in `p` and adding 1 to it. Then the value stored in `T` is retrieved, and these two values are "sent" to

the function. The following example shows how to write and use a
function with a *non-empty* parameter list:

```
Using A Function Parameter List [ParamList.java]

public class ParamList
{
    static double calcAverage(int a, int b)
    {
        double result = 0.0;
        result = (a + b) / 2.0;
        return result;
    } // calcAverage

    public static void main(String[] argv)
    {
        int x = 100;
        int y = 200;
        double z = calcAverage(x, y);
        System.out.println(z);
    } // main
} // public class
```

Note that each input in the header's parameter list has a data type
and an identifier. The data type specifies what the value, variable,
or expression in the call has to conform to. Each identifier, **a** and
b, is a variable for use *inside* the function, initialized to the value
from the call, `calcAverage(x, y)`.

When the program starts at the first statement in main, and
the sequential processing of statements reaches the one with
the call, here is what happens. The values stored in **x** and **y**
are retrieved and used to initialize the values of **a** and **b** in the
function. Then the function's code is processed, and a value for
the variable `result` is determined. When the function ends,
it substitutes the value stored in `result` for the expression
`calcAverage(x, y)` in main. Then sequential processing
continues in main.

It is important to remember that parameters in calls are evaluated
as values, and they are used to initialize the variables in the
function's parameter list. That is why calls can have values,

variables, or expressions, because they all can be reduced to values before the call takes place.

Note how the variable names in main do not match those in **calcAverage** – they do not have to. It is not their names that determine how they transfer their values to the function – it is their location in the parameter list that does.

Also note that the setting of **result** to a default value of zero is not really necessary. In fact, the body of the function could be written any of these ways:

Alternative Ways To Write calcAverage	

`double result = 0.0; // a default`
`result = (a + b) / 2.0;`
`return result;`
	`double result = (a + b) / 2.0;`
	`return result;`

	`return (a + b) / 2.0;`

`double result; // no default needed`
`result = (a + b) / 2.0;`
`return result;`
	`return ((a + b) / 2.0);`

8.3 Void Functions

Sometimes functions produce their own output and do not need to return anything to main. In this case, the return type can be specified as **void** to indicate that there is no **return** statement. Here's a simplified example of what is called a "void function":

A Simple Void Function [Name.java]

```
public class Name
{
    static void outputName(String name)
    {
        System.out.println(name);
    } // outputName

    public static void main(String[] argv)
    {
        outputName("George Washington");
    } // main
} // public class
```

Actually, main itself is a void function, called by the computer's operating system to start running the program.

The most important thing to remember about void functions is that the call must be made as a *stand-alone statement* – it cannot be used as an expression in another statement. That is because it does not produce a value that can be substituted for the call. So the call statement looks like this: `outputName("George Washington");` . Note also that there is no `return` statement in the function, and no 3-step process like we have in value-returning functions.

Besides demonstrating how void functions work, this example also shows that text can be passed through a parameter list, and that actual values can be substituted for variables in a function call.

The next example shows how a function can be called more than once:

```
                    Using Void Functions [Addition.java]

import java.io.*;

public class Addition
{
   static void additionProblem(int topNumber, int bottomNumber) throws Exception
   {
      BufferedReader cin;
      cin = new BufferedReader(new InputStreamReader(System.in));

      int userAnswer;
      System.out.print("\n\n\n      " + topNumber + " + " + bottomNumber + " = ");
      userAnswer = new Double(cin.readLine()).intValue();

      int theAnswer = topNumber + bottomNumber;
      if (theAnswer == userAnswer)
         System.out.println("       Correct!");
      else
         System.out.println("       Very good, but a better answer is " + theAnswer);
   } // additionProblem

   public static void main(String[] argv) throws Exception
   {
      additionProblem(8, 2);
      additionProblem(4, 8);
      additionProblem(3, 7);
      additionProblem(4, 10);
      additionProblem(11, 2);
   } // main
```

Note the text containing three `\n`s. "Backslash-N" inside quoted text is another was to skip to the next line besides using several `println`'s.

8.3.1 Using `return` In Void Functions

While value-returning functions *do* have to end with a `return` statement, void functions do *not*. So it's unusual to see `return` in a void function.

But to exit a void function before reaching the end of it, you can use the simple statement `return;`, without specifying a return value.

8.3.2 Randomizing Functions And Game Programming

The math problems in the above example are specified by the programmer. Every time the program runs, it presents the same 5 problems. It would be nice if the computer could choose the numbers for the problems at random!

Java provides a "random number generator". To randomly "draw" a whole number with a value between 0 and 9, inclusive, use this expression:

```
(int)(10 * Math.random())
```

Each result is equally probable. Add 1 to the above in order to get numbers in the range 1 to 10, inclusive. Here's how to simulate the roll of a six-sided die:

```
1 + (int)(6 * Math.random())
```

Here's how to simulate the roll of two six-sided dice:

```
(1 + (int)(6 * Math.random())) + (1 + (int)(6 * Math.random()))
```

The purpose of `(int)` is explained in chapter 9.

8.4 Some Examples With Functions

Here are some examples with functions. You can copy, save, and compile them. You can modify them and see how they work. Make sure that you understand everything in each of these examples.

8.4.1 Input Validation Example

Here's an example of a validating input loop in a function:

An Input Validation Function [YesNo.java]

```java
import java.io.*;

public class YesNo
{
  static String getAnswer() throws Exception
  {
    String result = "";

    BufferedReader cin;
    cin = new BufferedReader(new InputStreamReader(System.in));

    while (true)
    {
      System.out.print("Your answer [yes/no]: ");
      result = cin.readLine();
      if (result.equals("yes")) break;
      if (result.equals("no")) break;
      System.out.print("Let's try this again. ");
    } // while

    return result;
  } // getAnswer

  public static void main(String[] argv) throws Exception
  {
    // do stuff...
    if (getAnswer().equals("yes"))
    {
      // do stuff...
    } // if
  } // main
} // public class
```

8.4.2 A Password-Protected Program

Here's an example that shows how to password-protect a program:

```
A Password-Protected Program [Password.java]

import java.io.*;

public class Password
{
  static void getPassword() throws Exception
  {
    BufferedReader cin;
    cin = new BufferedReader(new InputStreamReader(System.in));

    while (true)
    {
      String password;
      System.out.print("Enter the password: ");
      password = cin.readLine();
      if (password.equals("12345")) break;
      System.out.print("INVALID. ");
    } // while
  } // getPassword

  public static void main(String[] argv) throws Exception
  {
    getPassword();
    // do stuff...
  } // main
} // public class
```

8.4.3 Void vs Value-Returning

Here is an example that converts the void function in **Addition.java** into a value-returning function in order to keep score. Some programmers will write a value-returning function where a void function would otherwise do, so that it can return a *result code*. A result code value of zero usually indicates success. Any other value can be used as an error code.

In the example below, a value of one is returned if the answer is correct, so that it can be added to the score in main.

Using A Value-Returning Function Instead Of Void [KeepingScore.java]

```java
import java.io.*;

public class KeepingScore
{
  static int additionProblem(int topNumber, int bottomNumber) throws Exception
  {
    int result = 0; // 0 is the code for incorrect

    BufferedReader cin;
    cin = new BufferedReader(new InputStreamReader(System.in));

    int userAnswer;
    System.out.print("\n\n\n       " + topNumber + " + " + bottomNumber + " = ");
    userAnswer = new Double(cin.readLine()).intValue();

    int theAnswer = topNumber + bottomNumber;
    if (theAnswer == userAnswer)
    {
      System.out.println("        Correct!");
      result = 1; // 1 is the code for correct
    } // if
    else
      System.out.println("        Very good, but a better answer is " + theAnswer);

    return result;
  } // additionProblem

  public static void main(String[] argv) throws Exception
  {
    int score = 0;
    score += additionProblem((int)(10 * Math.random()), (int)(10 * Math.random()));
    score += additionProblem((int)(10 * Math.random()), (int)(10 * Math.random()));
    score += additionProblem((int)(10 * Math.random()), (int)(10 * Math.random()));
    score += additionProblem((int)(10 * Math.random()), (int)(10 * Math.random()));
    score += additionProblem((int)(10 * Math.random()), (int)(10 * Math.random()));

    System.out.println("\n        TOTAL SCORE: " + score + " out of 5");
  } // main
} // public class
```

Note that the above example also puts in the random element, so that the problems are different every time the program runs. Also note that it introduces a shorthand way to write `score = score + ...;`, which is `score += ...;`. (Actually, since the 5 statements in main are exactly the same, we could have put in a count-controlled loop and written the statement only once!)

The `+=` operator introduced in the above example has some relatives. Here is a list of some useful shorthand operators, by example:

Shorthand Operator Example:	...Is Shorthand For:
score += 1;	score = score + 1;
score -= 1;	score = score - 1;
result *= 10;	result = 10 * result;
average /= n;	average = average / n;

8.5 Classic Computer Science Solutions

The two classic problems introduced in chapter 6 lend themselves well to solutions with functions. We still have to get to chapter 11 to complete these solutions, but we can move closer to them here.

8.5.1 Classic Min/Max Solution In A Function

The classic problem of finding the minimum and/or maximum values from among multiple values can be solved with functions. This lets the details of the logic be removed and reused. Here are some code blocks that show how this is done:

```
Finding The Maximum Or Minimum Value
static int getMaxValue(int a, int b, int c)
{
    int result = a;
    if (result < b) result = b;
    if (result < c) result = c;
    return result;
}

static int getMinValue(int a, int b, int c)
{
    int result = a;
    if (result > b) result = b;
    if (result > c) result = c;
    return result;
}
```

To extend this to 4 or more values, just add more parameters and more if-statements.

8.5.2 Classic Sorting Logic

The classic problem of reordering multiple values from lowest to highest (or the reverse) can also be handled with functions. While we need to get through chapter 11 before we can fully deal with this problem, we can get closer here.

Sorting Values Lo-to-Hi

```
static void sortValues(int a, int b, int c)
{
  // move the lowest value to "a"
  if (a > b)
  {
    int temp = a;
    a = b;
    b = temp;
  }
  if (a > c)
  {
    int temp = a;
    a = c;
    c = temp;
  }

  // move the next lowest value to "b"
  if (b > c)
  {
    int temp = b;
    b = c;
    c = temp;
  }

  // output the reordered values
  System.out.println("" + a + ',' + b + ',' + c);
}
```

Since the parameter values are shared with the function as *copies* of their original values, the originals in the call statement are not affected. This function can be adapted to variables of other data types, as well.

8.6 Exercises, Sample Code, Videos, And Addendums

Go to www.rdb3.com/java/8 for extended materials pertaining to this chapter.

Chapter 9. Counting On Your Fingers: Bits And Bytes

What you need to know about computer memory is how numbers and text are stored, which will help you understand why numbers and text are treated separately in programming. You also need to understand why there is a distinction between whole numbers and floating point numbers, and to know that there are *range limits* for numbers and that there is a *precision issue* with floating point variables.

We know that computers can store values, including numbers and text – even audio and video. But just how do they do that, anyway? This chapter explains how computers store values, and in so doing, shows why computers make the distinction between whole numbers and floating point numbers. And in case you've been thinking that all we need is the `double` data type and why should we ever use `int`, this chapter will help you see the value of `int`.

You will also learn that there are other data types for whole numbers besides `int`, and why floating point numbers can be either `float` or `double`. It all has to do with range and precision – something you might not have expected of a computer. Aren't computers supposed to be "accurate"? Well, it turns out that there are limitations, and all programmers need to be aware of these.

9.1 Computer Memory: Vast Arrays Of On/Off Switches

If you study the "memory" of a computer – what's inside those SD cards, memory sticks, and DDRs – you will find that they consist of millions or billions of electronic on/off switches. That's it – nothing more than on/off switches. Each switch can store one of two possible values – off or on – zero or one.

A switch is called a *bit*, and it is made out of several electrical components – resistors and transistors combined in a circuit. By applying an electrical pulse to the circuit that comprises one bit, it can be placed into one of two possible states, which represent "on" and "off".

So how can a computer store a number, which has many more than two possible values? Well, remember when you learned to count on your fingers? Each finger can be held up or down to represent on or off. By combining all ten fingers of both hands, you could group fingers in various ways to represent numbers in the range of 0 to 10. Computers do something like this.

9.1.1 Bits And Counting

Computers group bits together in order to get past the zero-one range limitation. Just like our hands group our fingers in sets of five, computers (typically) group bits in sets of eight – a set of 8 bits is called a *byte*.

On the fingers of one hand you learned to count from zero to five, and so you might think that a byte can be used to count from zero to eight. But computer designers realized that we were not using our 5 fingers very efficiently. Consider this: there are multiple ways to represent the number *two*, depending on which two fingers you hold up – what a waste! What if every possible combination of fingers held up or down represented a different number? There are 32 (that is, 2 x 2 x 2 x 2 x 2) unique combinations, ranging from all fingers down to all fingers up. We could actually count from 0 to 31 on the fingers of one hand, if we assigned a unique number to each unique finger configuration. (Pinky-up could be 1, ring-finger-up could be 2, pinky-up and index-finger-up could be 9, etc.) Extend this idea to two hands, and we can count to over 1000 – now that's efficiency!

Here's how to do this: assign the value 1 to your pinky, 2 to your ring finger, 4 to your middle finger, 8 to your index finger, and 16 to your thumb. (The key is to start with 1 and double it each time). For any finger held up, add its value to the total. For example, pinky and ring finger both up is 3 (that is, 1 + 2). (Since some up-down finger combinations are painful or impossible, you might try holding your open hand over a flat surface, and touching the surface to represent "up" – it's easier and faster to do.)

9.1.2 Bits And Negative Numbers

So our hand can simulate a byte of computer memory, and store numbers from 0 to 31 or more, depending on how many hands we use. But what about negative numbers? There is one obvious solution – use one finger to track whether the number is positive or negative – a "sign bit". But this idea is just a little bit wasteful, because it results in two ways to represent zero – plus zero and minus zero! A *better* solution is to make the largest bit represent the *negative* of its normal value. That is, let the thumb in a one-hand number be -16 instead of +16. Then all fingers except the thumb up represents 15 (that is, 1 + 2 + 4 + 8), thumb up only represents -16, thumb and pinky is -15, etc.

If we were to use two hands, the 16 thumb would go back to +16, and the thumb of the *second* hand would go negative (-512, actually).

Whole numbers are done this way in computers. The whole number data type `int` uses 4 bytes for a total of 32 bits in *most* of today's Java compilers. It can represent numbers in the range -2,147,483,648 to 2,147,483,647. The reason that computer languages have additional data types for whole numbers besides `int` is that the other data types use different numbers of bytes, and therefore have different ranges!

9.1.3 To Infinity And Beyond: Whole Numbers And Range Limitations

Remember when you first learned the concept of infinity? You can always add 1 to a number and get the next largest number, and continue doing so forever! Not so with computers – no matter how many bytes they use to store a number, they eventually reach a limit. To force the issue, let's try a program that starts with a value close to the limit for `int`, and add 1 to it several times:

Going Beyond Infinity [BeyondInfinity.java]

```
public class BeyondInfinity
{
  public static void main(String[] argv)
  {
    // 2 less than the maximum int
    int a = 2147483645;

    int i;
    for (i = 0; i < 5; i++)
    {
      a++;
      System.out.println(a);
    } // for
  } // main
} // public class
```

```
output:  2147483646
         2147483647
         -2147483648
         -2147483647
         -2147483646
```

Whole number values that would exceed the maximum limit wrap to the lower limit and continue from there. Similarly, values that would be below the minimum limit wrap to the upper. *(Note that commas are not allowed in whole number values in computer languages!)*

9.1.4 Range Limitations For Whole Number Data Types
There are multiple whole number data types in Java – they vary in the number of bytes used in memory for a variable, and the range of values they can store.

Whole Numbers		
Data Type	Memory Used	Range Of Possible Values
byte	1 byte	-128 to 127
short	2 bytes	-32,768 to 32,767
int	4 bytes	-2,147,483,648 to 2,147,483,647
long	8 bytes	-9,223,372,036,854,775,808 to 9,223,372,036,854,775,807

So we can represent whole numbers in computer memory, even though they are range-limited and have no concept of infinity. But what about *fractions*?

9.2 Floating Point Numbers

The use of bytes to represent numbers does not address fractional values. There's a 1 and a 2, but what about 1½? What about 3.14159265? A solution is to modify the bit-counting approach so that instead of representing whole numbers, we represent fractional values instead. That is, the pinky's value is ½, ring finger is 1, index finger is 2, etc. – or we could start with ¼ or less for the pinky. This is *almost* what the computer does, and for this to work, there needs to be a second set of data types – ones whose first bit is a fraction instead of 1. (Actually, the value of the first bit varies, depending on the size of the value being stored – for example, why stop at ¼ if the number stored is only 10?)

Floating Point Numbers			
Data Type	Memory Used	Range Of Possible Values	Precision (Digits)
float	4 bytes	approx. -10^{30} to -10^{-30}, 0, and 10^{-30} to 10^{30}	6 or 7
double	8 bytes	approx. -10^{300} to -10^{-300}, 0, and 10^{-300} to 10^{300}	15 or 16

Here's the important thing about floating point numbers – it's the last column in the table above – *precision*. If computers are so accurate, why are we talking about precision? Consider the case where the pinky value is ½. We can only represent values *to the nearest half*. And even though the first bit in a floating point representation is effectively a lot smaller than ½, the problem remains – there is *no continuum of numbers* on the computer's number line! So if we divide our hand-held number of 1½ by two, we should get ¾ – but we cannot divide numbers finely enough to show the ¼ value – we have ½ and 1, and that's as close as we can get to ¾. We end up *rounding off* the true number to one that is as close as we can get in computer's numbering system. Try the following code block for yourself:

```
// try this in Java
double x = 3;
String precision = "#.00000000000000000000";
System.out.println(new DecimalFormat(precision).format(x));
System.out.println(new DecimalFormat(precision).format(x + 0.0000000000000000001));
System.out.println(new DecimalFormat(precision).format(x + 0.000000000000001));
```

If you write the above code block into a program you should see that the first two console output statements yield the same result, even though the second one adds a small amount to the variable. But the third output statement *does* show an effect on the variable. This is because the small amount added in the second output statement is below the *precision* range for the data type **double**. But the small amount added in the third output statement is just inside the precision range, so it shows up.

Precision is an issue for floating point numbers, but not for whole numbers. *That is why we need separate data types for both* – so we can choose the precision of whole numbers at the expense of fractional capabilities, or choose the fractional capabilities of floating points at the expense of precision. It's an age-old result of the way computers work, and is *not* particular to Java – it's due to the fact that computers count on their "fingers".

9.2.1 Output Precision vs Floating Point Precision
Wait a minute – we were able to specify the precision for **x** in the last example with **new DecimalFormat(precision)**. Shouldn't that give the programmer some control over this issue of precision? Well, obviously not, judging by the results of the example! It turns out that **new DecimalFormat(precision)** simply directs that the output be *displayed* with the number of decimal digits specified. If the number is stored with *less* precision than is asked for in the output, the computer "makes up" the digits that it does not know exactly! (It's better than generating a error and terminating the program at that point.)

Try this – the loops *should* each cycle 10 times. But one of them actually goes on forever!

More Round-Off Error	
This Stops When It Should.	**This Does Not!**

`double x;`
`for (x = 0; x != 2.5; x += 0.25)`
`  System.out.println(x);`
	`double x;`
	`for (x = 0; x != 1; x += 0.1)`
	`  System.out.println(x);`

9.3 Representing Characters

Bits are used in various combinations to represent whole numbers and floating point numbers. But what about characters and text? The solution is actually a simple one – numbers are used to stand for characters, and the *data type* distinguishes between the two. For example, the number 65 when stored in an `int` is 65, but when stored in the single-character data type `char`, it's `'A'`.

The data type `char` takes 2 bytes of memory in Java, which gives it enough bits for over 65 thousand unique combinations with which to represent letters of the alphabet, digits, and punctuation marks – enough to cover all the languages of the world! The first 128 in the sequence are called the "ASCII standard" characters. They include the English alphabet, and some European characters.

Text stored in `String` variables is actually a series of `char` variables. The number of bytes needed to store a `String` variable depends on the number of characters of text stored in it. There is one `char` per character, including spaces (ASCII code 32), plus one special character to mark the end: a *null* (ASCII code 0). So even empty text has one character, the null!

In case you are wondering, ASCII stands for "American Standard Code for Information Interchange". You may also be wondering since characters are represented by numbers, what happens if you add or subtract from a `char` variable? That is, for `char c = 'A';`, what does the expression `c++` do? It advances the character to the next one in the ASCII sequence, `'B'` (code 66)! So the following code block outputs the alphabet:

```
The English Alphabet
char c = 'A';
for (c = 'A'; c <= 'Z'; c++)
   System.out.print("" + c + ' ');
System.out.println();
```

9.4 The True/False, Yes/No, On/Off, Up/Down, Left/Right Data Type

There is another data type that is separate from numbers and text. It is the only thing that a bit can represent by itself: two exact opposites. Ironically, since bits are grouped as bytes in computer memory, it still takes a whole byte's worth of bits to do this. After all, to use just one finger, you still have to involve a whole hand! This data type is a "Boolean".

Booleans are used as "flags". The data type name is Java's **boolean**, and its two possible values are **true** and **false**. No, there are not any "yes", "no", "left", or "right" values – you just have to decide which of a pair of opposites is to be represented by **true** and which is **false**.

For example, we will search through sets of data in following chapters, and we will use the **boolean** data type to tell whether or not we found a specific value in the data set. Here's an incomplete sample code block:

```
A Boolean Flag
boolean found = false;
while (true)
{
    ...
    if (...) found = true;
    ...
} // while
if (found)
    ...
```

Booleans also offer a more straightforward way of writing 8.4.3's **KeepingScoreBoolean.java**:

```
                Using A Boolean As A Return Type [KeepingScoreBoolean.java]

import java.io.*;

public class KeepingScoreBoolean
{
    static boolean additionProblem(int topNumber, int bottomNumber) throws Exception
    {
        boolean result = false; // assume answer will be wrong

        BufferedReader cin;
        cin = new BufferedReader(new InputStreamReader(System.in));

        int userAnswer;
        System.out.print("\n\n\n        " + topNumber + " + " + bottomNumber + " = ");
        userAnswer = new Double(cin.readLine()).intValue();

        int theAnswer = topNumber + bottomNumber;
        if (theAnswer == userAnswer)
        {
            System.out.println("        Correct!");
            result = true; // answer is right!
        } // if
        else
            System.out.println("        Very good, but a better answer is " + theAnswer);

        return result;
    } // additionProblem

    public static void main(String[] argv) throws Exception
    {
        int score = 0;
        if (additionProblem((int)(10 * Math.random()), (int)(10 * Math.random())))
            score++;
        if (additionProblem((int)(10 * Math.random()), (int)(10 * Math.random())))
            score++;
        if (additionProblem((int)(10 * Math.random()), (int)(10 * Math.random())))
            score++;
        if (additionProblem((int)(10 * Math.random()), (int)(10 * Math.random())))
            score++;
        if (additionProblem((int)(10 * Math.random()), (int)(10 * Math.random())))
            score++;

        System.out.println("\n        TOTAL SCORE: " + score + " out of 5");
    } // main
} // public class
```

9.5 Literal Values

Values written directly into code are called *literal values*. Depending on how they are written, they have a data type associated with them. For example, whole numbers are of data type int (like 0, 100, or -1). Floating point numbers are of data type double (like 0.0, 3.14159, or -40.0).

Literals are usually base 10 numbers, but whole number literals can also be octal (base 8) or hexadecimal (base 16). To write a number as base 8 octal, prepend a zero (like 011, which is the same as decimal 9, or 077 which is the same as decimal 63 – 7 eights plus

7 ones). Note that 08 and 09 are undefined and will cause compiler errors, because the digits 8 and 9 do not exist in base 8. To write a number as base 16 hexadecimal, prepend 0x (like `0xFFFF` or `0xABCD1234`). Note that A through F are digits added to the base 10 set of 0 through 9 in order to get 16 digits for the base 16 numbering system.

Literal `float` values are written by appending uppercase or lowercase F (like `3.14159f` or `100.0F`). Longs are written by appending uppercase or lowercase L. Literal `char` values are written as single characters, with single-quotes (or apostrophes) before and after (like `'A'`). Literal `String` values are written as any number of characters, with quote marks before and after (like `"Hello"`). Literal `boolean` values are `true` and `false`.

9.6 Type Casting

Computer languages have a variety of data types, and for each variable in your program you have to decide which data type to use. Also, the data type for the result of a math operation depends on the data types of the values in the operation. Here's the problem: if you have 3 `int` values (for example, `a`, `b`, and `c`) and you want their average, the expression `(a + b + c) / 3` will truncate (that is, lose) the fractional part of the result, because that is what whole number division does. That means `(1 + 1 + 2) / 3` is *not* one and a third – it's one!

The solution to this problem is *type casting*. You can write code that *forces* type casting – this is a way to *temporarily* convert a value of one type into a related type, such as an `int` to a `double`. Here's how:

Type Casting In Expressions
```
int a = 100;
int b = 17;
int c = -29;
double average1 = (a + b + c) / 3; // LOSES THE FRACTIONAL RESULT
double average2 = (double)(a + b + c) / 3; // that's better
double average3 = (a + b + c) / 3.0; // this works, too
```

Remember the `(int)(10 * Math.random())` Java expression from the previous chapter? That uses type casting to convert a floating point value into an integer value, dropping any fractional portion.

9.7 Exercises, Sample Code, Videos, And Addendums

Go to www.rdb3.com/java/9 for extended materials pertaining to this chapter.

Chapter 10. Interactive Programs: File I/O

Input can be gathered from a variety of sources. In chapters 3 and 4 we specified input values directly in the program listings. Then in chapter 5 we learned how to get values from a user via the `cin` object. In this chapter we learn how to get user-typed input from a text file, so a user can stage their input values in advance of running the program, and save and edit them in a file. The same techniques can be applied to save the scores in computer games – how many wins and how many losses!

10.1 Text File Input

Text files are like typing responses to console prompts, but doing so in advance and storing them in a file. It's remarkably easy to convert console input to text file input. Actually, you can "mix-and-match" file and console input in the same program, so that there can be some of each. For example, you could use console input for a user to type the name of a text file, and then get the rest of the input from that text file.

But there are two important differences between console input and text file input. Prompts are not necessary for text file input – remember, the responses are typed in advance and stored in a text file. So the user has to know the program pretty well in order to know what to reply *before* the questions are asked! Another difference is that the *name* of a file has to be specified, and your program has to "open" the file.

You do not have to deal with "error handling" when using console I/O, but you do with file I/O because things can go wrong with files that can't go wrong with keyboards. For example, a specified file may not exist, or it may not be complete. So we will learn the basics of file error handling – enough to get by.

The coding requirements for text file input are these: (1) type the proper Java **import** statement, (2) replace **cin** with its text file equivalent, **fin**, (3) "open" a file, and (4) add error handling.

10.1.1 The File I/O Library
At the top of the code listing, insert this:

```
import java.io.*;
```

10.1.2 The **fin** Object
Actually, this does not have to be named **fin** – it just has to be any valid identifier. But in any case, **fin** is another "object", and by now you may have noticed that some objects already have names, like **System.out**, and others we have to name ourselves. Here's what to insert somewhere in the body of main, before any other reference to **fin** *(remember sequential processing!)*:

```
BufferedReader fin;
```

The above statement reserves the identifier **fin** to be used for reading one or more text files. In the same way that the same variable identifier cannot be declared more than once, the same is true of **fin**.

10.1.3 Opening A Text File For Input
"Opening" a file makes an exclusive, read-only attachment of a specified file to your program. This attachment continues until your program "closes" the file or ends. Here is how to open a specified file:

```
fin = new BufferedReader(new FileReader("data.txt"));
```

Then after the last reference to **fin**, when you are finished reading from the file, use this statement to close the file:

```
fin.close();
```

In the above, the name of the file to be opened is **data.txt**. It is expected to exist in the *working* folder. You can specify that a file be located in any other folder by including the folder specification in front of the filename, like this *(note the forward slash **/** – some systems also allow a backslash, but it has to be written as a double-backslash:* ****):

```
fin = new BufferedReader(new FileReader("e:/Programming class/data.txt"));
```

The filename does *not* have to end in **.txt**. It can be anything, including **.ini** or no filename extension at all. The only requirement is that it be a text file – one that is editable and viewable using any text editor. The other type of file is "binary" – that's left for future study.

The filename can be specified using a **String** variable instead of a filename written in quotes, like this:

```
String fileName = "e:/Programming class/data.txt";
fin = new BufferedReader(new FileReader(fileName));
```

Since you can use a text variable to specify the filename in an "open" statement, that makes it possible to prompt the user to type the name of a file:

```
String fileName;
System.out.println("What file do you want to use for input? ");
fileName = cin.readLine();
fin = new BufferedReader(new FileReader(fileName));
```

Note that you may include a folder specification for a file when you type it in response to a prompt. Use either a universally understood slash **/** or a Windows backslash **** to separate parent and child folders – you do *not* have to use double-backslash as you would do if you typed the filename in your code.

To read a file a second time, close it and open it again. Here's how to reopen the same file, or use **fin** to open a different file:

```
fin.close();
System.out.println("What file do you want to use for input next? ");
fileName = cin.readLine();
fin = new BufferedReader(new FileReader(fileName));
```

Here's a handy table of interchangeable code blocks for opening a text file for input, summarizing the preceding discussion:

```
                    fin = new BufferedReader Variations

// open a specifically named file, data.txt, in local folder
fin = new BufferedReader(new FileReader("data.txt"));

// open a specifically named file, data.txt, in some other folder
fin = new BufferedReader(new FileReader("e:/Programming class/data.txt"));

// open a file whose name is stored in a String variable
String fileName = "e:/Programming class/data.txt";
fin = new BufferedReader(new FileReader(fileName));

// open a file whose name is entered by the user
String fileName;
System.out.println("What file do you want to use for input? ");
fileName = cin.readLine();
fin = new BufferedReader(new FileReader(fileName));

// open a 2nd file (storing the filenames in a String variable)
fin.close(); // be sure to close 1st file before opening 2nd
System.out.println("What file do you want to use for input next? ");
fileName = cin.readLine();
fin = new BufferedReader(new FileReader(fileName));
```

10.1.4 Error Handling

File error handling is required in Java. The purpose of writing error-handling code is to tell the computer what to do *in case* there is a problem with file I/O. To accommodate possible file I/O errors append this expression **throws Exception** to the **public static void main** statement. This causes the program to terminate in case the file does not exist. Some operating systems, such as Windows, may require that the user press CTRL-C in order to return to the command prompt after such errors.

10.1.5 Bringing It All Together: File Input Coding

Here is an example that converts section 5.1's **ItsAboutYou.java** program to use file input:

Transferring Values From A Text File [ItsAboutYou2.java]

```java
import java.io.*;

public class ItsAboutYou2
{
    public static void main(String[] argv) throws Exception
    {
        // open aboutYou.txt for input
        BufferedReader fin;
        fin = new BufferedReader(new FileReader("aboutYou.txt"));

        // read an int from one line of an input file
        int age;
        age = new Double(fin.readLine()).intValue();

        // read a double from one line of an input file
        double gpa;
        gpa = new Double(fin.readLine()).doubleValue();

        // read a String from one line of an input file
        String name;
        name = fin.readLine();

        // read a char from one line of an input file
        char gender;
        gender = fin.readLine().charAt(0);

        fin.close();
    }
}
```

An Input File [aboutYou.txt]

```
46
3.9
George Washington
M
```

Of course, the above program produces no output. But by leaving out this detail, we can focus on text file input coding. Note how similar it is to console input – one uses `cin` and the other uses `fin`. Also note the differences – text file input requires that the filename be specified in an `open` statement.

In file input, the statement that "reads" an input value also skips to the next input value in the file – that is, it reads it sequentially. There is no need to write any code to advance to the next input value, because this happens automatically. There is also no going back or skipping forward – not easily, anyway. The most straightforward way to go back to a previous input is to close and reopen the text file.

10.1.6 End-Of-File Loops

To process *all* of the input in a text file without knowing in advance the number of lines in the file, there needs to be a way to detect when the end of the file is reached. To test for end-of-file, use this statement: `if (!fin.ready() break;`. Here's an example that reads a whole text file named **readFile.txt** and outputs its contents to the screen.

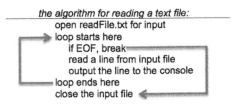

the algorithm for reading a text file:

```
open readFile.txt for input
loop starts here
    if EOF, break
    read a line from input file
    output the line to the console
loop ends here
close the input file
```

Reading A Text File With A End-Of-File Loop [ReadFile.java]

```java
import java.io.*;

public class ReadFile
{
  public static void main(String[] argv) throws Exception
  {
    BufferedReader fin;
    fin = new BufferedReader(new FileReader("readFile.txt"));

    while (true)
    {
      if (!fin.ready()) break;
      String lineFromFile;
      lineFromFile = fin.readLine();
      System.out.println(lineFromFile);
    } // while
    fin.close();
  } // main
} // public class
```

In the above example, the if-break is the *very first statement* in the loop. When this is the case, you can write the loop a bit more concisely by moving the if-break logic into the `while` statement, like this:

Another Form Of An End-Of-File Loop

```
while (fin.ready())
{
    String lineFromFile;
    lineFromFile = fin.readLine();
    System.out.println(lineFromFile);
} // while
```

Note that the logic that was in the if-break gets *reversed* in the **while** statement. That's because the if-break said "if there are *no* lines left to read, exit the loop". But the **while** statement now says "if there *are* lines left to read, continue the loop".

10.2 Text File Output

Sending output to a text file is a lot like sending it to the console screen. The included library is the same as for text file input. The error handling code is the same as for text file input. Also, the name of the output text file must be specified, as it must for text file input.

10.2.1 The **fout** Object

As with **fin**, this does not have to be named **fout** – it just has to be any valid identifier. Here's what to insert somewhere in main, before any other reference to **fout**:

```
PrintWriter fout;
```

This creates an object named **fout** to be used for writing one or more text files.

10.2.2 Creating A Text File

When specifying a filename to receive output, the file may either already exist or not. If you specify a file that already exists, the file will be discarded and overwritten *without warning*. If the file does not already exist, this process creates it. In most operating systems it will appear in the file listing as soon as it is opened for output, but its size may be reported as zero until it is closed or the program ends. Here is how to open a named file:

```
fout = new PrintWriter(new FileWriter("data.txt"));
```

Then after the last reference to **fout**, when you are finished writing to the file, use this statement to close the file:

```
fout.close();
```

In the above, **data.txt** will be created (or recreated) in the *working* folder. As with input files, you can specify that a file be located in any other folder by including the folder specification in front of the filename. Also, the filename does *not* have to end in **.txt**. The text file that is written by your program will be editable and viewable using any text editor.

Overwriting of files is useful if you are keeping score in a game, or saving the state of a program for later restart at the same position. For example, a tic-tac-toe game may save the number of wins, losses, and ties in a text file. Upon starting the game, the program could read the file and display the win-loss history. While playing the game, the win-loss history is updated by new wins and losses. Then when the program ends, it can then replace the old win-loss history file by overwriting it.

Here is an example that uses a text file to keep score. To keep it simple, the program itself does not control the game being played – it just keeps score:

PROGRAMMING CONCEPTS IN JAVA

The Score-Keeping File [scores.txt]
10 3

sample contents:
  #of wins
  #of losses

Keeping Score [KeepingScore2.java]

```java
import java.io.*;

public class KeepingScore2
{
  public static void main(String[] argv) throws Exception
  {
    // open scores.txt (see text section 10.2.2)
    String scoreFile = "scores.txt";
    BufferedReader fin;
    fin = new BufferedReader(new FileReader(scoreFile));

    // create a variable, read it from scores.txt (10.1.5)
    int wins;
    wins = new Double(fin.readLine()).intValue();
    System.out.println("You won " + wins + " time(s).");

    // create a variable, read it from scores.txt (10.1.5)
    int losses;
    losses = new Double(fin.readLine()).intValue();
    System.out.println("You lost " + losses + " time(s).");

    // close scores.txt (10.1.3)
    fin.close();

    // play the game(s) in a loop here (MISSING)
    // ...for each win, do wins++;
    // ...for each loss, do losses++;

    // rewrite scores.txt with the latest scores
    PrintWriter fout;
    fout = new PrintWriter(new FileWriter(scoreFile));
    fout.println(wins);
    fout.println(losses);
    fout.close();
  }
}
```

The above program uses a text variable **scoreFile** to store the name of the text file. This is an alternative to typing the exact same name twice, in the two file opening statements (one for input and another for output). It is good programming practice to store a recurring value in a variable and use the variable instead of repeating the value.

Study the above code listing, because there are some subtleties – see if you can identify and understand each:

Blank lines are used to separate blocks of code, making it easier for humans to read – it makes no difference to the compiler.

- Variables are declared just before they are used, instead of putting all of them at the top of main – this is by programmer preference, as some programmers do put them all together at the top.
- The `.close()` statements appear as soon as they possibly can. This is not important for `fout.close()`, because the program ends after that anyway. But it is important that `fin.close()` appear before attempting to open `fout`, because otherwise the file remains exclusively attached to the `fin` object and the `fout` would fail.
- Both `System.out` and `fout` are used because there is output to both the console and a file.
- The file output statements skip to the next line after sending their output to the file – is this important? What would happen if they did not skip to the next line?
- This code listing is rather long and complicated. If there were any typing mistakes, what would the compiler errors look like? Try making some errors and see for yourself – you could leave out the Java library imports, semicolons, or open statements, etc. Note that some errors get by the compiler and do not show up until you run the program.

Here's a handy table of interchangeable code blocks for opening a text file for output:

```
                    C++ fout = new PrintWriter Variations

// open a specifically named file, data.txt, in local folder
fout = new PrintWriter(new FileWriter("data.txt"));

// open a specifically named file, data.txt, in some other folder
fout = new BufferedReader(new FileReader("e:/Programming class/data.txt"));

// open a file whose name is stored in a String variable
String fileName = "e:/Programming class/data.txt";
fout = new PrintWriter(new FileWriter(fileName));

// open a file whose name is entered by the user
String fileName;
System.out.println("What file do you want to use for input? ");
fileName = cin.readLine();
fout = new PrintWriter(new FileWriter(fileName));

// open a 2nd file (storing the filenames in a String variable)
fout.close(); // be sure to close 1st file before creating 2nd
System.out.println("What file do you want to use for input next? ");
fileName = cin.readLine();
fout = new PrintWriter(new FileWriter(fileName));
```

10.2.3 Appending To A Text File

By default, any existing text file is discarded and overwritten when you open it for output. But it is possible for your program to *append*, or add to an existing file instead of overwriting it. This is useful if you are building a database of transactions, for example, where each new transaction gets saved to a file. Here is how to open an output text file for appending instead of overwriting:

```
fout = new PrintWriter(new FileWriter("data.txt", true));
```

In the above, if the file does not already exist, it is created, as it would have been without the specification to append. Here is an example of using a text file to append output – it is a program that builds a class roster:

```
                 Appending Output To A Text File [ClassRoster.java]

import java.io.*;

public class ClassRoster
{
  public static void main(String[] argv) throws Exception
  {
    BufferedReader cin;
    cin = new BufferedReader(new InputStreamReader(System.in));

    // read a student's name from the keyboard (see 5.1)
    String name;
    System.out.print("What is your name? ");
    name = cin.readLine();

    // write the student's name to classRoster.txt
    PrintWriter fout;
    fout = new PrintWriter(new FileWriter("classRoster.txt", true));
    fout.println(name);
    fout.close();
  }
}
```

Note the change in the file open statement that specifies that the output file be appended to, instead of overwritten. Compile and run the program, and note that the output file is created the first time you run the program – you do not need to create it in advance! (By the way, this applies to any and all of the `fout = new PrintWriter` code block variations!)

By introducing logic in your programs, they can behave differently depending on circumstances. For example, in the class roster program above, what if the user enters a blank name (by pressing ENTER without typing their name first)? If this is the case, the program should not add the blank name to the text file. Or what if the name is a duplicate of a name already in the **classRoster.txt** file? Again, the program should not add the name. What if the **scores.txt** does not exist when you run the keeping-scores program from the previous chapter? Wouldn't it be better for the program to continue, setting the numbers of wins and losses both to zero, rather than terminating with an error?

Here's an example that modifies the class roster program:

```
                    Testing A True/False Condition
if (name.length() > 0)
{
    // open a file for output and write to it
    PrintWriter fout;
    fout = new PrintWriter(new FileWriter("classRoster.txt", true));
    fout.println(name);
    fout.close();
}
```

The **>** means "is greater than". Remember that **.length()** gets the number of characters stored in a **String** variable. So this expression tests "if the number of characters stored in the variable **name** is greater than zero, then use the code contained in the curly-braces."

10.3 Exercises, Sample Code, Videos, And Addendums

Go to www.rdb3.com/java/10 for extended materials pertaining to this chapter.

PART 3: Processing Data

Chapter 11. Checking It Twice: Arrays
11.1 Array Variables
11.2 Array Processing
11.3 Dynamically-Sized Arrays
11.4 Arrays In Function Parameter Lists
11.5 Arrays And Functions Together
11.6 Exercises, Sample Code, Videos, And Addendum

Chapter 12. Using Objects
12.1 Object Specifications
12.2 Objects
12.3 Arrays Of Objects
12.4 Objects And Functions
12.5 Object-Oriented Programming
12.6 Exercises, Sample Code, Videos, And Addendums

Chapter 13. Keeping a List: Array-Based Lists
13.1 Array-Based Lists
13.2 Other Ways To Make Lists
13.3 An Array-Based List Example
13.4 Exercises, Sample Code, Videos, And Addendums

Chapter 14. Lists Of Unlimited Size: Linked Lists
14.1 The Next-Link
14.2 The Start-Link
14.3 Building A Linked List
14.4 Traversing Linked Lists
14.5 A Linked List Example
14.6 Linked Lists Of Whole Numbers
14.7 Exercises, Sample Code, Videos, And Addendums

Chapter 15. Some Advanced Topics
15.1 The Easy Way: Collections
15.2 Functions That Call Themselves: Recursion
15.3 Where Do We Go From Here?

Chapter 11. Checking It Twice: Arrays

An "array" is a variable that can store more than one value *at the same time*. The variables that we have studied up to now can also store more than one value, but only one at a time. Whenever such a variable is set to a new value, the previous value is lost – only the *last* value is ever remembered. But not so for an array – it can remember a sequence of values. What you need to know about arrays is how to declare them, how to copy values into them and retrieve them later, how to "traverse" them, and how to use them with functions.

Consider this problem – we want to get the average of a series of numbers stored in a text file. That's not too hard:

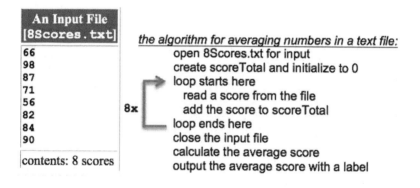

An Input File
[8Scores.txt]
66
98
87
71
56
82
84
90
contents: 8 scores

the algorithm for averaging numbers in a text file:
open 8Scores.txt for input
create scoreTotal and initialize to 0
loop starts here
    read a score from the file
8x   add the score to scoreTotal
loop ends here
close the input file
calculate the average score
output the average score with a label

```
                Averaging Numbers In A Text File [AvgFile.java]

import java.io.*;

public class AvgFile
{
  public static void main(String[] argv) throws Exception
  {
    // open 8Scores.txt for input
    BufferedReader fin;
    fin = new BufferedReader(new FileReader("8Scores.txt"));

    // read the scores and build the sum
    int scoreTotal = 0;
    int i; // loop counter
    for (i = 0; i < 8; i++)
    {
      int aScore;
      aScore = new Double(fin.readLine()).intValue();
      scoreTotal += aScore;
    } // for
    fin.close();

    // calculate and print the average
    double average = scoreTotal / 8.0;
    System.out.println("The avg of 8 numbers is " + average);
  } // main
} // public class
```

But what if we want to modify the program to count the number of scores that are *greater than the average*? We would have to reopen the file and re-read it, which is possible, but there has to be a better way. (Fortunately the numbers are read from a text file instead of the keyboard – it would be *really* hard to ask a user to re-enter all of the data!)

The solution is to *store each individual value* as it is read from the file (or from the keyboard) in the memory of the computer. Then we can access them again and again, as often as we wish, without going back to the original source of the data. For this, computer languages have array variables.

11.1 Array Variables

An array is a variable that can hold more than one value by the same name. It uses an "index" to distinguish among the many values stored in it. Here's how to create an array variable – an "array" for short – showing its conceptual representation:

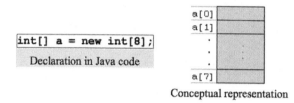

Conceptual representation

This variable **a** can store 8 **int** values at the same time! The first value is referenced as a[0] and the last as a[7], using "square brackets" around the index number. You say these as "a of zero" and "a of seven". Each of these is called an "element" of the array. They are used like any other **int**, for example:

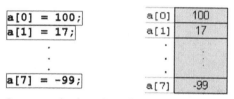

Representation in code   Conceptual representation

The array index value can be expressed not only as a value, but also as a variable (or an expression that results in a whole number). This means it can be used in a count-controlled loop, using the loop counter as an index. It's as if arrays and for-loops were made for each other!

Before we look at some details, let's consider this solution to the averaging problem posed above:

the algorithm for finding the number of scores greater than the average:
open 8Scores.txt for input
create an array to store 8 scores
loop starts here
   read a score from the file
   store the score in the array
loop ends here
close the input file

**An Input File
[8Scores.txt]**

66
98
87
71
56
82
84
90

contents: 8 scores

8X

create scoreTotal and initialize to 0
loop starts here
   retrieve a score from the array
   add the score to scoreTotal
loop ends here
calculate and output the average score

8X

create nGreater and initialize to 0
loop starts here
   if score from the array is > average score
     add 1 to nGreater
loop ends here
output nGreater with a label

8X

Finding The Number Of Scores Greater Than The Average [AvgFile2.java]

```java
import java.io.*;

public class AvgFile2
{
  public static void main(String[] argv) throws Exception
  {
    BufferedReader fin;
    fin = new BufferedReader(new FileReader("8Scores.txt"));

    // read and save the scores
    int[] score = new int[8];
    int i; // loop counter
    for (i = 0; i < 8; i++)
    {
      score[i] = new Double(fin.readLine()).intValue();
    } // for
    fin.close();

    // find the average
    int scoreTotal = 0;
    for (i = 0; i < 8; i++)
    {
      scoreTotal += score[i];
    } // for
    double average = scoreTotal / 8.0;
    System.out.println("The average of 8 numbers is " + average);

    // count #of scores > average
    int nGreater = 0;
    for (i = 0; i < 8; i++)
    {
      if (score[i] > average) nGreater++;
    } // for
    System.out.println("" + nGreater + " scores are greater than the average.");
  } // main
} // public class
```

There's a lot going on here, so let's take a look.

There are three successive loops in this program. Each is its own code block, separated by blank lines and headed by a comment line. The first loop simply reads the values from the file and stores them.

The second loop totals the elements of the array. Actually, the first and second loops could have been combined and done as one loop! The third loop runs through the saved scores and compares each to the average, counting those greater. (The for-loops have curly-braces as a container for their code blocks. For the code blocks that consist of one line, the curly-braces are *not necessary* – same as if-statements.)

11.1.1 Array Size

The "array size" is the number of elements in the array. In our examples, the size of the array named `score` is 8. When a Java array is created, the values initially stored in those 8 elements are zeroed out. The data type for the elements of an array can be any valid data type.

The size of a Java array can be retrieved in an expression from the array name itself, like this: `score.length`. It is better to use this, rather than repeating the number "8" throughout the code. If we ever wanted to change the number of scores to be processed, it could be a lot of work to track down all the 8's, and that kind of editing is prone to error. So in the examples that follow, we will be using `.length`.

11.1.2 Array Traversal

The use of a for-loop to process each element of an array is called "traversal". This is the powerful thing about using arrays. Arrays let us store large numbers of values easily, and for-loops let us process them easily.

Here's how you would traverse an array and set all of its elements to zero – of course, they start out as zero in Java, but you can set them to any other value as well:

```
Traversing An Array To Set Its Values To Zero
int[] a = new int[8];
...
int i;
for (i = 0; i < a.length; i++)
  a[i] = 0;
```

Note that the size of the Java array named "a" is retrieved as `a.length`, without parentheses (not to be confused with `.length()` that retrieves the length of a `String`). Java arrays track their size.

Here's how you would traverse an array and set all of its elements via the keyboard:

```
Traversing An Array To Set Values Via The Keyboard
int[] a = new int[8];
int i;
for (i = 0; i < a.length; i++)
{
   System.out.print("Please enter a[" + i + "]: ");
   a[i] = new Double(cin.readLine()).intValue();
} // for
```

Here's how you would traverse an array and send its values to the console for output:

```
Traversing An Array To Output Its Values
int i;
for (i = 0; i < a.length; i++)
  System.out.println("a[" + i + "] = " + a[i]);
```

11.1.3 Curly-Brace Initialization

When Java arrays are created, the values of their elements are zeroed out. But it is possible to specify the values of each element upon declaration. It's called "curly-brace initialization" and it is done like this:

```
int[] daysPerMonth = new int[]{31, 28, 31, 30, 31, 30, 31, 31, 30, 31, 30, 31};
```

Note that the array size is not specified in the square brackets. Instead, the computer *counts* the number of elements and makes the array exactly that size.

It can be used to reassign values to an array at a later time after declaration. The only difference in the statement is that the declaration part cannot be repeated. It would be like this (changing February from 28 to 29 days for leap year):

```
daysPerMonth = new int[]{31, 29, 31, 30, 31, 30, 31, 31, 30, 31, 30, 31};
```

Of course, it would have been easier to do
daysPerMonth[1] = 29; in this case, since only one value changed. Also, even though it is in this case, the size of a reassigned array does not have to match the size of the original array.

11.2 Array Processing

Arrays are processed by traversal. In traversal, you access each element of the array, one-by-one, for assignment, output, or any other operation. Some more advanced types of array processing involve searching and sorting.

11.2.1 Searching An Array

The **AvgFile2.java** program from earlier in this chapter actually contains examples of searching. The last loop traverses the array, looking for values greater than the average, and counts them. It provides a good model for searching, and can be applied to any number of situations. Here is that loop:

```
A Counting "Search Loop"
int nGreater = 0;
for (i = 0; i < score.length; i++)
    if (score[i] > average) nGreater++;
```

Here is what you should notice about this "search loop" – these are things common to all search loops: First, a variable is declared above the loop, which stores the piece of information we want from the search. But it is set to the wrong value (presumably): zero! It looks like we know the answer in advance, wrongly so, by saying that it is zero. But it is actually just a starting point – it is zero *before* we start our search and until we find otherwise. In other words, until we look at the array's elements, let's just *assume* that the answer is zero. If we find this to be incorrect, we can reset it later.

Next, we traverse the array. Inside the for-loop's code block, there is a test of a single element to see if it matches our search criterion. If it does, we adjust the variable that is *now* seen to have been incorrectly set to zero. We continue to adjust this variable's value as we inspect and test each element. When the loop completes, the variable now contains the correct value.

The variable **nGreater** is called an "accumulator". It is a variable that gets set to an assumed value *before* the search loop starts, and gets adjusted inside the loop. **scoreTotal** in the same example is also an accumulator – it is assumed to be zero, and adjusted as each element is inspected.

Here is another example that finds whether or not there are any perfect scores. Two possible ways are shown – one that takes less *processing time* and another that takes less *code*:

```
Two Boolean Search Loops
boolean hasPerfectScore = false;
for (i = 0; i < score.length; i++)
{
  if (score[i] == 100)
  {
    hasPerfectScore = true;
    break;
  } // if
} // for

// ...or this
boolean hasPerfectScore = false;
for (i = 0; i < score.length; i++)
  if (score[i] == 100)
    hasPerfectScore = true;
```

Both ways start out with an accumulator named **hasPerfectScore**, which we assume to be false (until proven to be true). The longer code block breaks out of the loop once a perfect score is found – there is no point in looking any further! The shorter code keeps looking even though it will not change the result, but it takes less code to write. (Sometimes programmers have to make decisions based on size vs. speed.)

11.2.2 Finding A Maximum Or Minimum Value

We can now complete the classic solution introduced in chapters 6, 7, and 8 – the one that finds the maximum or minimum value in a set of values. Here are some code blocks that show how this is done:

```
Finding The Maximum Or Minimum Value
// find the maximum
int max = score[0];
for (int i = 1; i < score.length; i++)
  if (max < score[i]) max = score[i];

// find the minimum
int min = score[0];
for (int i = 1; i < score.length; i++)
  if (min > score[i]) min = score[i];

// find maximum AND minimum
int max = score[0];
int min = score[0];
for (int i = 1; i < score.length; i++)
{
  if (max < score[i]) max = score[i];
  if (min > score[i]) min = score[i];
} // for
```

Note that the accumulators are initialized to the first element of the array. That is because until we look beyond the first element, as far as we know, it is the maximum and the minimum – the *only* value. The for-loop starts with `i = 1` instead of zero – that's because there is no point in comparing the first element to itself. It would not hurt to start at 0 instead of 1, though.

11.2.3 Sorting An Array With A Code Block

We can also complete the other classic solution introduced in chapters 6 and 8 – the one that *rearranges* the elements of an array so that they are in numerical order, low-to-high or high-to-low. The same applies to an array of `String`s, which may be arranged in alphabetical order, or perhaps in the order of the shortest to the longest text. You can sort arrays using a code block, or using a library function. Both ways are shown here. For variety, these examples use arrays of text.

Sorting Text In Alphabetical Order [`StringSort.java`]

```java
public class StringSort
{
  public static void main(String[] argv)
  {
    String day[] = new String[]{"Monday",
      "Tuesday", "Wednesday", "Thursday",
      "Friday", "Saturday", "Sunday"};

    System.out.print("Unsorted: ");
    int i;
    for (i = 0; i < day.length; i++)
      System.out.print(day[i] + ' ');
    System.out.println();

    // 2 nested for-loops
    for (i = 0; i < day.length; i++)
    {
      int j;
      for (j = i + 1; j < day.length; j++)
      {
        if (day[i].compareTo(day[j]) > 0)
        {
          // swap code
          String temp = day[i];
          day[i] = day[j];
          day[j] = temp;
        } // if
      } // for
    } // for

    System.out.print("Sorted: ");
    for (i = 0; i < day.length; i++)
      System.out.print(day[i] + ' ');
    System.out.println();
  } // main
} // public class
```

Let's look at this sorting example more closely. First, the array is a text array with 7 values, initialized to the days of the week in chronological order. Next, there is a loop that traverses and outputs the array elements before they are sorted. Then there is a code block that uses *nested for-loops* – one inside the code block of another. Since i is already being used as a counter in the first (or *outer*) loop, we cannot use it again in the second (or *inner*) loop without creating lots of confusion! So a new counter, j, is introduced. The two loops work together to compare two elements of the array, and swap them if they are out of order with respect to one another. The three lines of code with the variable `temp` are what's called *swap code*, because it swaps the contents of two elements.

Note that the inner loop starts "j" with the value `i + 1` instead of zero. This is a critical feature of the sorting code block, and without this it would not work correctly.

The nested loops sort the text alphabetically, because of the statement `if (day[i].compareTo(day[j]) > 0)`. To sort in reverse alphabetical order, use `<` instead of `>`. In comparing text, remember that case matters. In the ASCII sequence, uppercase letters come before lowercase. So the word "Zebra" actually comes *before* "aardvark", since `'Z'` is ASCII code 90, and `'a'` is code 97. To make a case independent comparison, you could create temporary copies of `day[i]` and `day[j]`, convert the copies to uppercase, and compare the uppercased copies in the if-statement.

You could also compare based on text length instead of alphabetically. To do so, you would change the if-statement like this: `if (day[i].length() > day[j].length())`. If you did this for our particular case, note that there are several ties – 4 days have 6 letters in their names. Since we do not include in the if-statement how to handle ties, it's left to the computer to decide.

For sorting an array of `int`s named `a`, low-to-high, the if-statement would be: `if (a[i] > a[j])`. Change the `>` to `<` for high-to-low. The only other thing that would change for sorting `int`s is the data type of the `temp` variable – it must match the data type of the elements in the array.

Note that strings are not treated the same as other data types. The expression `s.compareTo(t)` returns a positive number, if the text stored in `s` comes alphabetically *after* that stored in `t`. For all other data types, use the greater-than operator: `i > j` -- just don't use it for strings.

11.2.4 Sorting An Array With A Library Function Call

The Java library function **Arrays.sort** sorts an array with one statement – no nested for-loops are required! Here's an example. For variety, the data is read from a file – the same text file from the start of this chapter.

```
                Sorting An Array Of ints [SortFile.java]

import java.io.*;
import java.util.*;

public class SortFile
{
  public static void main(String[] argv) throws Exception
  {
    BufferedReader fin;
    fin = new BufferedReader(new FileReader("8Scores.txt"));

    // read and save the scores
    int[] score = new int[8];
    int i;
    for (i = 0; i < score.length; i++)
      score[i] = new Double(fin.readLine()).intValue();
    fin.close();

    Arrays.sort(score);

    for (i = 0; i < score.length; i++)
      System.out.print("" + score[i] + ' ');
    System.out.println();
  } // main
} // public class
```

The single parameter in the **Arrays.sort(score);** statement is the array name to be sorted. There is an import required for using this function: **import java.util.*;**

11.3 Dynamically-Sized Arrays

When we declared the arrays earlier in this chapter, all were declared with a specific size known by the programmer before the program was compiled. The size of 8 for the array of scores read from the text file **8Scores.txt** had to match the number of scores in the file, or there would be a problem. It would be nice if the *first* line of the file could tell the program how many elements to have in its array.

174

Java allows the number of elements to be specified by a *variable*. Here is the statement to declare an array of **n** elements, where **n** is an **int** variable:

```
int[] score = new int[n];
```

This form of array declaration does also allow for curly-brace initialization.

Java allows the number inside the square brackets of an array declaration to be either a constant or a variable. So the problem of the 8-element array easily goes away by adding a count to the text file, reading it into a variable, and using that variable to declare the array instead of the number 8:

Using A Dynamic Array [DynamicArray.java]

```
import java.io.*;

public class DynamicArray
{
    public static void main(String[] argv) throws Exception
    {
        BufferedReader fin;
        fin = new BufferedReader(new FileReader("score.txt"));

        int size; // read from 1st line of the file
        size = new Double(fin.readLine()).intValue();
        int[] score = new int[size];

        // read and save the scores
        int i;
        for (i = 0; i < size; i++)
            score[i] = new Double(fin.readLine()).intValue();
        fin.close();

        for (i = 0; i < size; i++)
            System.out.print("" + score[i] + ' ');
        System.out.println();
    } // main
} // public class
```

An Input File [score.txt]
```
8
66
98
87
71
56
82
84
90
```

Note that after the file is opened, the number "8" is transferred from the first line of the file into the variable **size**, which is used to specify the array size.

Actually, any non-negative integer value can be used to create a dynamically sized array, including zero. Yes, it is possible to have an array of size zero in Java! It may not seem like that would ever be useful, but it can be, although we will not consider such cases in this text.

11.3.1 Multiple Values From A Single Line Of Input

In chapters 5 and 10, we showed how to capture values entered from the keyboard or read from a text file. But we could only enter one value at a time (that is, each followed by the ENTER key), or have one value per line in the text file. Using dynamic arrays, it is possible to read an array of values from a single line of input! Here are some code examples, using **fin**, but they could just as well use **cin** instead.

Getting Multiple Values From A Single Line Of Input:
Reading An Array Of Values In Java

```
String[] line = fin.readLine().split("[ ]");
int[] age = new int[line.length];
for (int i = 0; i < line.length; i++)
  age[i] = new Double(line[i]).intValue();
```

```
String[] line = fin.readLine().split("[ ]");
double[] gpa = new double[line.length];
for (int i = 0; i < line.length; i++)
  gpa[i] = new Double(line[i]).doubleValue();
```

```
String[] name;
name = fin.readLine().split("[ ]");
```

```
String[] line = fin.readLine().split("[ ]");
char[] gender = new char[line.length];
for (int i = 0; i < line.length; i++)
  gender[i] = line[i].charAt(0);
```

In these examples, the values are separated by a *single space*, as specified between the square brackets of the **split** call. For tab-separated values, use **.split("[\t]")**, and for comma-separated use **.split("[,]")**.

11.4 Arrays In Function Parameter Lists

Array variables can be shared with functions by using the parameter list, much like other variables. But before we see how this is done, there is one major difference that programmers need to be aware of. When **int** variables are shared with functions, or variables of other basic data types, *copies* are made. So if the copy gets changed in the function, it does not affect the original. This is called "pass by value".

But when an *array* is shared with a function, no copies are made – instead, the *original* array is shared. Any changes made to the elements of the array inside the function *do* affect the original array! This called "pass by reference" .

To specify an array in the parameter list, use a data type that matches the elements of the array, but append a **[]** symbol. In the following example, an array of **int**s is shared with a function whose job is to return the average of the elements in the array:

```
                      An Averaging Function

static double getAverage(int[] score)
{
  double result = 0; // set to default value

  int sum = 0;
  for (int i = 0; i < score.length; i++)
    sum += score[i];
  result = (double)sum / score.length;

  return result;
} // getAverage

public static void main(String[] argv) throws Exception
{
  ...
  System.out.println("Average = " + getAverage(score));
  ...
} // main
```

Try adding this code to any of the preceding programs that have a **score** array, to track the array size as **score.length**. Note that the array name is the same in main and in the function – this is by programmer choice and it is *not* a requirement. Even though they both refer to the exact same array, it's okay to have different names, or *aliases*, for the same array in different scopes.

11.5 Arrays And Functions Together

To show how arrays and functions work together, let's rewrite **AvgFile2.java** with functions. One of the functions will be used to read the file, fill the array, and send the array back to main. In so doing, the details of getting values for the array are left to a *function*, as are the details of averaging the values and sending them to the console screen as output.

Arrays And Functions Together [AvgFile3.java]

```java
import java.io.*;

public class AvgFile3
{
  static void readScores(int[] score) throws Exception
  {
    BufferedReader fin;
    fin = new BufferedReader(new FileReader("8Scores.txt"));

    // read and save the scores
    for (int i = 0; i < score.length; i++)
      score[i] = new Double(fin.readLine()).intValue();
    fin.close();
  } // readScores

  static double getAverage(int[] score)
  {
    double result = 0;
    int scoreTotal = 0;
    for (int i = 0; i < score.length; i++)
      scoreTotal += score[i];
    result = (double)scoreTotal / score.length;
    return result;
  } // getAverage

  static int countScoresGreater(int[] score, double x)
  {
    int result = 0;
    for (int i = 0; i < score.length; i++)
      if (score[i] > x) result++;
    return result;
  } // countScoresGreater

  public static void main(String[] argv) throws Exception
  {
    int[] score = new int[8];
    readScores(score);
    double average = getAverage(score);
    System.out.println("The average of "
      + score.length + " numbers is " + average);
    System.out.println("" + countScoresGreater(score, average)
      + " scores are greater than the average.");
  } // main
} // public class
```

The above example contains several "design considerations", or programmer choices, which could have been done any number of ways. Let's discuss why things are done the way they are in the example code:

11.5.1 To Throw Or Not To Throw...
In Java, the "main" and "readScores" functions have `throws Exception`, but the other functions do not. Sometimes `throws Exception` is required in order to compile and other times it is not. When it is not required, it is the programmer's choice whether or not to include it. In the case of the above example, the choice was to exclude it if not needed, so as not to confuse new programmers studying this code.

Appending `throws Exception` is required in "readScores" because file input is used in the subprogram's code block. It is further required by "main" because it calls "readScores".

11.5.2 Local Variables In Functions
The `result` variables that are declared inside the value-returning functions are called "local variables", because they each belong to their own function. They are in separate scopes, and are therefore separate and distinct variables. They only exist while the program is executing the code in their function.

`fin` and `scoreTotal` are also local variables.

Also note that `i` is declared separately in every loop. While there are ways to share one counter variable among all loops, such as making it a *global* variable, it is better for each loop to have its own. The `i`'s are local to their loops – they are even more limited in their scope than `fin` and `scoreTotal`.

11.5.3 Parameter List Variable Names
The second parameter in `countScoresGreater` is named `x` in the parameter list, but the call in main has a variable named `average` in that position. The names do not match, and they do not have to. Whether the names refer to separate copies values from main, or it they are aliases for arrays in main, the *names* are local to their functions. In the same way, a person can go by two different names – one at work and another at home – array

180

variables can, too. Array variables have *aliases* across function scopes.

The reason for using a generic name like **x** in the function is to make **countScoresGreater** more generic. There is really no reason that it cannot be used to count the number of scores greater than *any* value – not just the average. By writing it as generic as possible, it is available to be used for other things, such as counting the number of A's (scores greater than 89).

11.5.4 Temporary Variables
The variable **average** in main is used to store the result of the **getAverage** call. It is really not needed, though, because **average** could be replaced where it appears in the two output statements with **getAverage(score)**. But doing so would require that the averaging loop be executed twice, which is a bit of a waste. So programmers generally will use an extra "temporary variable" to store the result of a call that is used multiple times.

Note that this was not done with **countScoresGreater**, because it is only called once.

11.5.5 Pass By Reference
In **readScores**, array elements are assigned values. Since arrays are *passed by reference*, the function gets the *original* version of the array, and any changes made to it affect main where the array was declared. This would not be so for anything that is not an array – **int**s and **double**s are *passed by value*, meaning that the function has a *copy* of the original value. Any change made to a copy in the function does not affect the original in main.

11.5.6 Array As A Return Type

The data type for an array has the square-bracket symbol in it, like **int[]**. It's okay to create a Java array and return it from a function.

```
Returning An Array

int[] getArrayOfInts(int size)
{
  int[] result = new int[size];
  ...
  return result;
}

int main()
{
  ...
  int[] a = getArrayOfInts(10);
  ...
}
```

11.6 Exercises, Sample Code, Videos, And Addendums

Go to www.rdb3.com/java/11 for extended materials pertaining to this chapter.

Chapter 12. Using Objects

Like the array, an "object" is a variable that can store multiple values at the same time. But unlike arrays, the values in an object do not have to all be the same thing, like all scores or all temperatures or all names. An object can store all the values associated with, for example, a student's school record, like their name as text, their ID as a whole number, and their grade-point-average as a floating point – all in one variable called an *object*.

Actually, the Java array *is* an object, too, but it's got that special restriction about all values being the same thing, so array objects get a special syntax (square-bracket indexing) that takes advantage of that. Other objects don't get to use the square-bracket syntax. They use the dot syntax, like arrays' `.length`, as we'll soon see.

Objects can be visualized as database records, which may have multiple data items, or "fields", such as name, address, city, state, and zip code. Such data does not lend itself very well to single-value variables, because you'd have to use a separate variable for each field. That's fine, but what if you are working with multiple records? Now you need arrays for each field, and you have to manage each one. If you want to use functions, you have to list each field separately in the parameter list, and if you ever add *more* fields, you have to change *all* the parameter lists.

12.1 Object Specifications

The first thing you have to do in order to use objects is to decide which data type to use for each field in the object. For our example, let's consider a student's school record as an object, with fields for name, student ID, and grade point average. We could add a lot more to this, but let's keep it simple for the sake of learning.

The name is text and should be represented with the `String` data type. Student ID is a 7-digit number and could be represented as a `String` or `int`. No math operations will be done with student IDs, and it can be hard to represent leading zeros with an `int`, so a `String` is a good choice – but let's go with `int` for instructional purposes. Grade point average has a fractional part, so let's use `float`. We could use `double`, but we don't need 15 digits of accuracy and we've not used `float` up to now, so let's go with `float`. As you can see, there are design considerations that go into the selection of data types for fields – it's not always obvious.

Besides data types, each field needs a "field name". These have to be valid Java identifiers, like variable names and function names. Let's use `name`, `id`, and `gpa`. Also, the whole structure needs an identifier – let's use `Student`. Here is how all of this gets put together in code, and what it represents conceptually:

```
class Student
{
    String name;
    int id;
    float gpa;
} // Student
```

Representation
in Java code

table: Student		
name	id	gpa

Conceptual representation

Conceptually, an "object specification" represents an empty data table, with each row able to represent one record, and each column representing a field. Note that just defining an object is like typing column headings – rows containing values will be added later, as the table starts out empty.

The object specification appears inside the curly-brace container headed by the `class` keyword. It goes is *below* the `import` statement(s), and *above* the `public class`. It actually defines a *new data type*, which you can now use in the rest of your program below its specification, so be careful not to choose an identifier that exactly matches any data type of the language (like `String`).

The Java compiler creates a separate **.class** file for each class that you define -- in this case, **Student.class**. So if you ever decide to change the name of a class in your code, be sure to delete its previously-created **.class** file (if any). And avoid naming your classes the same as a class in a Java library that you may wish to use someday – yours will supercede Java's!

You can use any previously defined data type for a field in your object specification – even one defined by yourself, as long as it appears above.

12.2 Objects

The whole idea of writing a specification for an object is so there can be single variables and arrays of variables that can hold all of these data fields for each record individually. Once specified, you can use your new data type in the same way you use other data types, except for assignment and retrieval of field values, which is a new thing. So you can declare them, specify them as return types, include them in parameter lists, and make arrays of them.

12.2.1 Object Declarations
Here are declaration statements that can go in any code block, and a conceptual picture of initially empty records being added to the data table:

```
Student x = new Student();
Student y = new Student();
```

table: Student		
name	id	gpa

This is not exactly how other variables are declared for data types that are part of the language, like **int** and **String**. Those declarations consist of a data type specification followed by an identifier, like **int age;** .

12.2.2 Using Object Data Fields
But there are some things you cannot do with objects, such as use one directly in a **System.out** statement. The computer does *not* know to format an object and represent it in output.

The Java language provides the "dot operator" to get to a specific field by its identifier. For example, for a **Student** object named **a**, the way to get to the name of the student is **a.name**. Likewise, the remaining fields are **a.id** and **a.gpa**. Each of these behaves exactly like the data type that it is, so to get the length of student **a**'s name, use **a.name.length()**. (Don't let the double "dot operators" worry you – they are applied in their order of appearance, left to right). To set **a**'s grade point average, use for example **a.gpa = 3.67;** .

```
// creating two objects
Student a = new Student();
Student b = new Student();
```

```
a.name = "George";
a.id = 17890;
a.gpa = 3.67;
```

```
b.name = "John";
b.id = 17970;
b.gpa = 3.53;
```

table: Student		
name	id	gpa
a	George	17890	3.67
b	John	17970	3.53

Field values can also be read directly from a text file. To read object **a**'s ID from a file, use:

```
// reading data into an object
a.id = new Double(fin.readLine()).intValue();
```

To show object **a** on the console screen, do something like this:

```
// sending object fields to the console screen
System.out.print("Name=" + a.name);
System.out.print(", ID=" + a.id);
System.out.print(", GPA=" + a.gpa);
```

You might think that **x = y;** assigns (or copies) all of the fields of "y" to "x", so that they are both the same, but in Java, it *makes "x" an alias for "y"*, and thereby totally loses track of the student formerly known as "x"!

12.3 Arrays Of Objects

Conceptually, an array of objects is like a spreadsheet table, with each row representing *one* object. With such an array in memory, you can do all kinds of things, including searching and sorting – anything you can do using a traversing for-loop. The code for an object array is a straightforward application of everything we already know. For example:

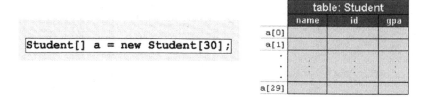

```
Student[] a = new Student[30];
```

The way to get to the name of the first student object is `a[0].name`. The remaining fields are `a[0].id` and `a[0].gpa`. The length of the first student's name is `a[0].name.length()`, which looks complicated, but is not so bad when you break it down into parts. To set the grade point average of the first student, use e.g., `a[0].gpa = 3.67;`. To read the first student's ID from a text file, use:

```
// reading arrayed object data
a[0].id = new Double(fin.readLine()).intValue();
```

But before you can use any of the objects of the Java array, you first have to do this: `a[0] = new Student();`. To initialize all elements of the array, use a loop, like this:

```
Initializing An Array
Student[] a = new Student[30];
for (int i = 0; i < a.length; i++)
   a[i] = new Student();
```

12.4 Objects And Functions

Objects can be used in functions just like any other variable.
They can be returned by value-returning functions, they can
be parameters, and they can be local variables. Except for one
syntax option that is presented here, there's no difference in how a
Student object and an **int** variable are treated.

12.4.1 Returning An Object From A Value-Returning Function
This example uses the standard value-returning function 3-step
structure, declaring a variable, setting its value, and returning it.
It's returned value gets stored in **s** in main:

Objects In Value-Returning Functions	

`static Student getGeorge()`
`{`
  `Student result = new Student(); // step 1`
  `...`
  `return result; // step 3`
`} // getGeorge`
	`public static void main(String[] argv)`
	`{`
	  `...`
	  `Student s = getGeorge();`
	  `...`
	`} // main`

12.4.2 An Object As A Function Parameter
The following example adds a void function with an object as its
parameter – note that it works just like any other parameter, except
that they are passed by reference, just like arrays.

Objects As Function Parameters	

`// newly added function`
`static void outputRecord(Student x)`
`{`
  `...`
`} // outputRecord`
	`public static void main(String[] argv)`
	`{`
	  `...`
	  `Student s = getGeorge();`
	  `...`
	  `outputRecord(s); // added call`
	  `...`
	`} // main`

The main reason for doing this is that objects can be large, and
for memory and efficiency reasons, it is better to avoid making
copies. Another reason is so that any changes made to the fields
of the object in the function affect the variable in main, because it
is an *alias* for the original object. Of course, we don't always want
our functions to change data fields in an object, but the efficiency
reason is reason enough to pass by reference. The following

example has an object with three **int**s, representing the time-of-day. It has a void function to output a variable of type **tod** in a nicely formatted way.

```
                  Time Objects [TodTest.java]

import java.text.*;

class tod
{
  int hour;
  int minute;
  int second;
} // tod

public class TodTest
{
  static void printTod(tod t)
  {
    System.out.print("" + new DecimalFormat("00").format(t.hour));
    System.out.print(":" + new DecimalFormat("00").format(t.minute));
    System.out.print(":" + new DecimalFormat("00").format(t.second));
  } // printTod

  public static void main(String[] argv)
  {
    tod noon = new tod();
    noon.hour = 12;
    printTod(noon);
  } // main
} // main
```

Note that for the **minute** and **second** data field values are not specified. All fields are initialized to zero in Java (or blanks, in the case of **String**s) when class variables are declared.

12.5 Object-Oriented Programming

There's actually a lot more to objects than has been covered in this book. In fact, "object-oriented programming" is a subject worthy of a full semester course in itself.

We've created our own objects by specifying data fields. But what about **cin** and **fin** and **fout** that we call objects? There certainly seems to be a lot more to those objects than our **Student** and **tod**. It turns out that you can define custom *behaviors* for objects, like **fin.open** – that tells the object to find and attach itself to a file. **String**s are objects, too – **s.length()** gets a **String** object named **s** to tell how many characters are stored in **s**.

We won't deal with behaviors in this book, except to use behaviors defined for objects that are already in the Java library. Defining our own behaviors is a topic left for future study.

12.6 Exercises, Sample Code, Videos, And Addendums

Go to www.rdb3.com/java/12 for extended materials pertaining to this chapter.

Chapter 13. Keeping A List: Array-Based Lists

What you need to know about array-based lists is that they are arrays in which not all of the elements are used, but are available for use in case they are needed. A new, separate `int` is used to track how many of the elements are actually in use at any time. Unlike previous chapters, the purpose of this chapter is *not* to train you in the use of this programming feature. It is instead an opportunity to introduce concepts that you will run into if you go further in your study of computer science, and to provide a way to practice the programming features we studied in preceding chapters.

A "list" is a collection of values – usually objects, but they can be whole numbers or floating points or text, too. The Java language allows the data types for these to be different from one another, even in the same collection! This concept is that of a "bag", which can contain lots of different items. But for purposes of our study in this book, we will consider collections of like data types only.

A list can be "empty" – that is, it can have zero values stored in it. Lists can grow in size by adding values, and shrink by taking them away. By contrast, the arrays that we studied in chapter 11 were of fixed, non-zero size, and each element had a value. So there are similarities and differences between arrays and lists. For example, with an array or a list, we could store test scores. But with a list we could find lowest test score and remove it, or add a new score for a late assignment.

There are several ways to represent lists in computers, and we will study these in this and the remaining chapters of this book. One way is to use arrays, and that's the subject of this chapter.

13.1 Array-Based Lists

Arrays are sized when they are created, and we normally consider all of their elements to be assigned valid values. An "array-based list" takes the idea of an array, but considers that the elements may not all be in use. The elements are placeholders for values that may or may not ever be assigned. The list's underlying array is divided into two parts – the front part, which has elements with assigned values, and the back part, which has elements in reserve for possible future use. To mark the dividing point, an **int** is used to track the number of elements that have valid, assigned values. It looks something like the figure below.

Conceptual representation

The variable **nNames** is the "list size". It not only tracks the number of elements in use at the time, but it also serves as a dividing line between valid, assigned elements, and as-yet unassigned. In the example, 3 elements are in use, the rest not (yet).

Here is what you need in order to declare array-based lists of various kinds, all initially empty: Note the naming convention used: the array names are not plural, so that **student[0]** is the first student object. The name of the list size variable is the same as that of the array, but plural, with a leading "n", and the first letter uppercased. The "list capacity" is named "MAX_" plus the uppercase, plural name of the array – it's the *array size* of the list's array.

A List Of Test Scores	
1 a size counter	`int nScores = 0; // initially empty list`
2 the array	`int[] score = new int[100];`
3 the maximum capacity	`score.length`

A List Of Names	
1 a size counter	`int nNames = 0; // initially empty list`
2 the array	`String[] name = new String[20];`
3 the maximum capacity	`name.length`

A List Of Student Records	
1 a size counter	`int nStudents = 0; // initially empty list`
2 the array	`Student[] student = new Student[30];`
3 the maximum capacity	`student.length`

13.1.1 Adding Values To A List

By default, new values are added at the end of the list. Here is the code for adding values to the ends of the lists created above:

Adding Values To A List

```
int aScore; // value to be added
... // set aScore's value
if (nScores < score.length)
   score[nScores++] = aScore;

String aName; // value to be added
... // set aName's value
if (nNames < name.length)
   name[nNames++] = aName;

Student aStudent = new Student(); // value to be added
... // set aStudent's field values
if (nStudents < student.length)
   student[nStudents++] = aStudent;
```

In the previous chapters, we loaded values directly into the array. But it's different with lists. We first store a new value in a temporary variable, like **aScore**. Then we check to see if the list is not full, and if it's not full, we copy the temporary variable's value into the next available position in the array.

Inside the square brackets of each assignment statement is the "post-increment operator", **++**, on the list size variable. What this does is to add one to the list size *after* the assignment takes place. The statement `score[nScores++] = aScore;` is the same as these two statements: `score[nScores] = aScore;` followed by `nScores++;`, but it is more concise. Also, as one statement, we avoid having to write a curly-brace container for the two statements that we'd need otherwise. It's not a big deal, but the more concise we can make things, the less room there is for error.

The following is a rewrite of an earlier example from chapter 11, but in this example the number of scores in the input file is *not* known in advance, and not stored in the input file's first line. Using a list, there is really no need to know the number of scores in the file in advance, and the program is protected against the possibility of there being too many scores to handle (that is, more than 100).

Reading An Unknown Number Of Values Into A List [ListFile.java]

```java
import java.io.*;

public class ListFile
{
  public static void main(String[] argv) throws Exception
  {
    BufferedReader fin;
    fin = new BufferedReader(new FileReader("many.txt"));

    // create an empty list of capacity 100
    int nScores = 0;
    int[] score = new int[100];

    // read and save the scores
    while (fin.ready())
    {
      // read a score from the file
      int aScore;
      aScore = new Double(fin.readLine()).intValue();

      // add score to list, if it's not full
      if (nScores < score.length)
        score[nScores++] = aScore;
    } // while
    fin.close();

    // find the average
    int i; // loop counter
    int scoreTotal = 0;
    for (i = 0; i < nScores; i++)
      scoreTotal += score[i];
    double average = (double)scoreTotal / nScores;
    System.out.println("The average of " + nScores
      + " numbers is " + average);

    // count scores > average
    int nGreater = 0;
    for (i = 0; i < nScores; i++)
      if (score[i] > average) nGreater++;
    System.out.println("" + nGreater
      + " scores are greater than the average.");
  } // main
} // public class
```

An Input File [many.txt]

```
66
98
87
71
56
82
84
90
98
84
67
63
80
81
99
```

Note that the first loop reads values from the file, until the end of the file is reached. The if-statement inside the loop protects against overfilling the array that supports the list. There is no error message in this example, in case the list capacity is exceeded – new values are simply read and ignored. But it would not be difficult to add code to either output a message or set a Boolean flag, as modeled in section 9.4.

13.1.2 Searching And Sorting A List

With array-based lists, the code for searching and sorting is almost the same as it was for the arrays we studied in chapter 11. The difference is that the *list size* is used for the end of count-controlled traversal loops instead of the *array size* (which is the same as the *list capacity*). So the counting search loop that counts the number of values greater than the average becomes this:

A Counting Search Loop For A List

```
int nGreater = 0;
for (i = 0; i < nScores; i++)
    if (score[i] > average) nGreater++;
```

Similarly, the Boolean search loop becomes this, even if **nScores** is zero:

Two Boolean Search Loops For A List

```
boolean hasPerfectScore = false;
for (i = 0; i < nScores; i++)
{
    if (score[i] == 100)
    {
        hasPerfectScore = true;
        break;
    } // if
} // for

// ...or this
boolean hasPerfectScore = false;
for (i = 0; i < nScores; i++)
    if (score[i] == 100)
        hasPerfectScore = true;
```

And for values of **nScores** other than zero, the value range search loops become:

Finding The Maximum Or Minimum Value Of A List

```
// find the maximum
int max = score[0];
for (i = 1; i < nScores; i++)
   if (max < score[i]) max = score[i];

// find the minimum
int min = score[0];
for (i = 1; i < nScores; i++)
   if (min > score[i]) min = score[i];

// find the max AND min
int max = score[0];
int min = score[0];
for (i = 1; i < nScores; i++)
{
   if (max < score[i]) max = score[i];
   if (min > score[i]) min = score[i];
} // for
```

To sort an array-based list, the sort function call is nearly the same as for a full array. There are 2 additional values in the Java parameter list, since the sorting does not involve the whole array: the integer zero, and the size counter. These tell the sort subprogram to sort only the first "nScores" values in the array, and to ignore everything after that.

Sorting A List Of ints [SortFileList.java]

```java
import java.io.*;
import java.util.*;

public class SortFileList
{
  public static void main(String[] argv) throws Exception
  {
    // open a file for input
    BufferedReader fin;
    fin = new BufferedReader(new FileReader("many.txt"));

    // create an empty list of capacity 100
    int nScores = 0;
    int[] score = new int[100];

    // read and save the scores
    while (fin.ready())
    {
      // read a score from the file
      int aScore;
      aScore = new Double(fin.readLine()).intValue();

      // save score to list, if not full
      if (nScores < score.length)
        score[nScores++] = aScore;
    } // while
    fin.close();

    Arrays.sort(score, 0, nScores);

    int i;
    for (i = 0; i < nScores; i++)
      System.out.print("" + score[i] + ' ');
    System.out.println();
  } // main
} // public class
```

An Input File [many.txt]

```
66
98
87
71
56
82
84
90
98
84
67
63
80
81
99
```

13.1.3 Functions And Array-Based Lists

When sharing an array-based list with a function, remember that there are now *two* values that identify the list – the array and the list size. So any function that receives the array in its parameter list also needs the list size. Here is an example:

An Averaging Function

```
static double getAverage(int[] score, int n)
{
  double result = 0;
  int i = 0;
  for (i = 0; i < n; i++)
    result += score[i];
  result = result / n;
  return result;
} // getAverage

public static void main(String[] argv) throws Exception
{
  . . .
  System.out.println("Average = " + getAverage(score, nScores));
  . . .
} // main
```

Note that the list size is passed to the program *by value*, meaning that the version in the function code block is a *copy*. So if you change it there, it will not affect the *real* size of the list.

13.1.4 Adding And Removing Values

While it is certainly possible to write code for adding values at positions in the list other than at the end, and to remove values, array-based lists do not really lend themselves very well to these operations. The problem is that such operations require mass movement of elements to create/close "gaps" in an array. There are better ways to represent lists, if you need features such as these.

But it is actually not hard to remove the *last* value in an array-based list – the index for its value is the list size minus one (for example, score[nScores - 1]). Then you would have to subtract one from the list size (using --nScores). Here is the code for removing the a value from the end of a list:

```
if (nScores > 0)
{
   int aScore = score[--nScores];
   ... // do something with the removed score
} // if

if (nNames > 0)
{
   String aName = name[--nNames];
   ... // do something with the removed name
} // if

if (nStudents > 0)
{
   Student aStudent = student[--nStudents];
   ... // do something with the removed object
} // if
```

In each of the above examples, a value is removed from the list (even though its "ghost" actually remains in the array!), and is copied to a new, temporary variable (like **aScore**) for further processing in the remainder of the if-statement code block (represented by "...").

13.2 Other Ways To Make Lists

Besides array-based lists, there are "linked lists" which do not use arrays at all, and there are library-based collection objects, which do most of the coding for you and provide a wide range of features. We study the code for linked lists in the next chapter, and collections in the chapter after that.

13.3 An Array-Based List Example

Here is an example of a list of student records, using the **class Student** from chapter 12. In the example, student objects are read from a text file, stored in a list, sorted, and sent to output. In a real program that processed student records read from a school's database, you would probably do more than simply sort and show the records, but that just adds more of the same to our example. So to avoid getting lost in the details, we'll just sort and show the records on the console screen.

An Input File [students.txt]	Processing Student Records In A List [StudentList.java]
George Washington 17890 3.25 ---------- John Adams 17970 4.0 ---------- Thomas Jefferson 18010 3.89 ---------- James Madison 18090 3.4 ---------- James Monroe 18170 3.53 ---------- John Quincy Adams 18250 4.00 ---------- Andrew Jackson 18290 3.27 ---------- Martin Van Buren 18370 3.10 ---------- William Harrison 18410 3.67 ---------- John Tyler 18411 3.39 ---------- James Polk 18450 3.91 ---------- Zachary Taylor 18490 3.95 ---------- Millard Fillmore 18500 3.7 ---------- Franklin Pierce 18530 3.77 ---------- James Buchanan 18570 3.42 ---------- Abraham Lincoln 18610 3.78 ---------- Andrew Johnson 18650 3.13 ---------- Ulysses Grant 18690 3.40 ----------	(see code)

```java
import java.io.*;
import java.text.*;
import java.util.*;

class Student
{
  String name;
  int id;
  float gpa;
} // Student

public class StudentList
{
  static void outputStudents(Student[] student, int nStudents)
  {
    String b = "                              ";
    int i;
    for (i = 0; i < nStudents; i++)
    {
      System.out.print("Name = " + student[i].name);
      System.out.print(b.substring(student[i].name.length()));
      System.out.print(" ID = "
        + new DecimalFormat("0000000").format(student[i].id));
      System.out.println(" gpa = " + student[i].gpa);
    } // for
  } // outputStudents

  public static void main(String[] argv) throws Exception
  {
    // open a file for input
    BufferedReader fin;
    fin = new BufferedReader(new FileReader("students.txt"));

    // create an empty list of capacity 100
    int nStudents = 0;
    Student[] student = new Student[100];

    // read and save the records
    while (fin.ready())
    {
      // create a record and read it from file
      Student aStudent = new Student();
      aStudent.name = fin.readLine();
      aStudent.id = new Double(fin.readLine()).intValue();
      aStudent.gpa = new Double(fin.readLine()).floatValue();

      fin.readLine(); // skip the ---------- separator

      // add record to list, if it's not full
      if (nStudents < student.length)
        student[nStudents++] = aStudent;
    } // while
    fin.close();

    // sort the students by name
    for (int i = 0; i < nStudents; i++)
    {
      for (int j = i + 1; j < nStudents; j++)
      {
        if (student[i].name.compareTo(student[j].name) > 0)
        {
          Student temp = student[i];
          student[i] = student[j];
          student[j] = temp;
        }
      }
    }

    outputStudents(student, nStudents);
  } // main
} // public class
```

Let's look at what just happened. Note that the input text file has
––––––––––– separating each student's data – this is to make
the file easier for humans to read. You see in main that there is
code to skip the separator.

The "compareTo" function is used to compare **String** variables,
low to high alphabetically, and case-dependent (so that all
uppercase letters come before all lowercase letters). The sort code
is based on student names, and since it uses "compareTo", it works
only for **String** fields! If you wanted to make the comparison
based on ID or gpa, you would rewrite the comparison with the
greater-than operator, used for variables that are not **String**s.
Here are alternate sort comparisons for the other, non-String fields
in **Student**:

```
if (student[i].id > student[j].id) // then swap
{
    Student temp = student[i];
    student[i] = student[j];
    student[j] = temp;
}
```

```
if (student[i].gpa > student[j].gpa) // then swap
{
    Student temp = student[i];
    student[i] = student[j];
    student[j] = temp;
}
```

The "outputStudents" function has two values in its parameter
list: the array and its associated size counter. In order to
print the name in a left-justified column of 30 characters, a
30-character **b** string variable is created, and the statement
`System.out.print(b.substring(student[i].name.length()));` follows the line that prints the name.
(To right-justify something, put that statement *before* the line that
prints the value that is to be right-justified.)

With all of the details moved to functions, "main" is pretty easy to
follow.

13.4 Exercises, Sample Code, Videos, And Addendums

Go to www.rdb3.com/java/13 for extended materials pertaining to this chapter.

Chapter 14. Lists Of Unlimited Size: Linked Lists

As in the previous chapter, the purpose of this chapter is *not* to train you in the use of linked lists. It is instead an opportunity to introduce concepts that you will run into if you go further in your study of computer science, and to provide an application of the programming features we studied in preceding chapters for the sake of practicing what you've just learned. So try to understand the "link" concept as you study this chapter, knowing that you will explore it in detail in future studies. Focus on the applications of variables, branching, loops, objects, and functions.

There are two problems with array-based lists: (1) they have a limited capacity, and (2) if you do not use them to their capacity, you've wasted memory. "Linked lists" solve the capacity problem. There is no limit specification! A limit was inherent in array-based lists, because a number needed to be used in the declaration of the array. But not so with linked lists! Also, there are no wasted elements in linked lists, because the list only contains values that were specifically linked in.

A drawback of linked lists is that they require that their values be *objects*. If you want a list of `int`s or `String`s, you have to put the `int` as a field in an object specification, which may only have that one field. This may seem like a lot of overhead and extra work, but in most applications, linked lists are used with objects anyway, so the object specification already exists in most cases, and all you do is add another field – a "next-link".

14.1 The Next-Link

The values contained in linked lists are objects. In order for an object to be suitable for use in a linked list, its object specification needs to contain a "next-link" to the next object. Mostly, objects do not have links in them – but objects intended for use in linked lists do. The next-link is normally the *last* field in the object specification, and it is usually named "next".

An Object Specification For Use In A Linked List

```
class Student
{
  String name;
  int id;
  float gpa;
  Student next; // the "next-link"
}; // Student
```

Objects containing a next-link are called "nodes"

14.2 The Start-Link

The identifier for a linked list is its "start-link". Here is how to declare an *empty* linked list:

```
Student start = null; // the start-link declaration
```

While it is not required, and some programmers and textbooks do not do so, linked lists should *always* start out empty. That's what the **null** does in the declaration statement.

By convention, the identifier for a linked list is named **start**. But if you have more than one list in the same scope, they obviously cannot have the same identifier, so other names can of course be used.

A value of **null**, which is a Java keyword, indicates that the list is *empty*. A value other than **null** would be the first node in the list.

14.3 Building A Linked List

Nodes can easily be added and removed anywhere in a linked list. But in this book we only show how to add and remove nodes to the *front* of a list, leaving other linked list features for future study.

14.3.1 Adding A Node To A Linked List

There are 3 steps to adding a node. The first is to *create* the node. The second is to *assign values* to the node's data fields – all but its next-link. The last is to *link the new node* into the list.

Here's the code for creating and adding a node:

```
Adding A Node To A List
// STEP 1: create a node
Student s = new Student();

// STEP 2: fill its data fields
s.name =...;

// STEP 3: add node to list
s.next = start;
start = s;
```

14.3.2 Removing A Value From A Linked List

Here's a simple code-block to remove the last-added value from the list, storing its value in a temporary object for processing.

```
Removing The Last-Added Node
Student aStudent = start; // remove node
start = start.next; // relink the linked list
```

14.3.3 Start-Links, Next-Links, And Nodes – Oh, My!

Okay, so the code for linked lists can be given to you as it has above, but what does it all really mean? Conceptually, arrays are fairly easy to understand. An array is like a classroom with students' desks all laid out in orderly rows. An array-based list is like filling those desks starting with the left-most one in the front-most row, and working to the right until the first row is filled, and then continuing to the next row. By keeping track of the number of students already in the room (using a list size variable), the instructor can *compute* the location of the desk to assign to the next-arriving student.

By contrast, a linked list is like a room with desks, tables, displays, and other structures scattered about. It starts out with an instructor, but no students, because they have not arrived yet.

When the first student arrives and chooses a desk, the instructor writes on an index card the *desk's* location in the room – not the student's name or ID, just there the *desk* is. When the second student arrives and chooses desk, the instructor *hands off* the index card to the newly arriving student – it's now the new student's job to track that. The instructor makes a new index card to track where the *new* arrival is, to replace the one given to the new student. This continues as more students arrive.

The instructor can always find all the students in the room because the instructor's index card notes where the last-arriving student is, and that student can direct the instructor to another student because it's written on the index card given to them by the instructor when they arrived. This continues until the first-arriving student is found, who has no index card.

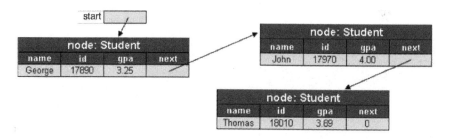

The instructor's index card is the *start-link*, noting where the last-arriving student can be found. Each student is a *node*, because besides having a name, ID, and other student-related data, they also have a *next-link* – the index card with where the student who arrived before them can be found. The *first-arriving* student has no index card.

14.4 Traversing Linked Lists

We use a for-loop to traverse arrays and array-based lists. We also use a for-loop to traverse linked lists. But the loop looks a bit different:

Traversing A Linked List

```
Student p;
for (p = start; p != null; p = p.next)
{
    ...
}
```

---

p is like an erasable index card in our classroom example above. It starts out with a copy of what's on the instructor's index card, **p = start**, and the first cycle of the loop uses that value – the location of the last-arriving student. After that cycle, the value on the **p** index card is scratched out and overwritten with what's on the last-arriving student's index card, **p = p.next**, and cycles continue until the cycle for the first-arriving student (without an index card) completes.

Inside the loop's curly-brace container, the fields are accessed with these expressions: **p.name**, **p.id**, and **p.gpa**. It looks something like this – note the addition of a box labeled "p":

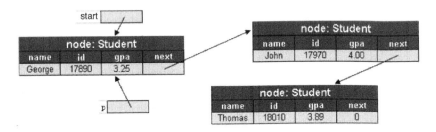

Conceptual representation

p starts out referring to the same node that **start** refers to, as depicted above where it points to George. This is accomplished in the code by the expression **p = start**. Then before the second cycle of the loop, it moves so that it refers to the second node in the list, and so on. Moving from one node to the next is accomplished in the code by the expression **p = p.next**. This continues until **p** finally reaches the last node and ends up with a value of **null**.

14.4.1 Getting The Size Of A Linked List

Array-based lists use **int**s to track their size and capacity. But not so with linked lists! While it is certainly possible to carry an **int** for linked list size, we're not doing so here. Here's how to find the size of a linked list – by traversing and counting:

```
Counting The Nodes In A Linked List
int size = 0;
Student p;
for (p = start; p != null; p = p.next)
   size++;
```

14.5 A Linked List Example

Here is **StudentList.java** rewritten using a linked list. There is no sorting. Linked list sorting is a bit complicated, and we leave that for future study. Also, functions are left out for simplicity's sake.

Processing Student Records In A Linked List [StudentLinkedList.java]

```java
import java.io.*;
import java.text.*;

class Student
{
  String name;
  int id;
  float gpa;
  Student next; // the link
} // Student

public class StudentLinkedList
{
  public static void main(String[] argv) throws Exception
  {
    BufferedReader fin;
    fin = new BufferedReader(new FileReader("students.txt"));

    // create an empty linked list
    Student start = null;

    // read and save the records
    while (fin.ready())
    {
      // create a node and read its data fields
      Student aStudent = new Student();
      aStudent.name = fin.readLine();
      aStudent.id = new Double(fin.readLine()).intValue();
      aStudent.gpa = new Double(fin.readLine()).floatValue();

      fin.readLine(); // skip the separator line

      // add node to front of list
      aStudent.next = start;
      start = aStudent;
    } // while
    fin.close();

    // traverse the list and print
    String blank = "                              ";
    Student p;
    for (p = start ; p != null; p = p.next)
    {
      System.out.print("Name = " + p.name);
      System.out.print(blank.substring(p.name.length()));
      System.out.print(" ID = "
        + new DecimalFormat("0000000").format(p.id));
      System.out.println(" gpa = " + p.gpa);
    } // for
    System.out.println();
  } // main
} // public class
```

14.6 Linked Lists Of Whole Numbers

As previously explained, you cannot have a linked list of **int**s or
Strings, without first enclosing them in an object. So here is an
example that reads whole numbers from the keyboard, stores them
in a linked list, and sends their average to the console display:

Putting Whole Numbers Into A Linked List [IntLinkedList.java]

```java
import java.io.*;

// a class created to store one int, plus the link
class Score
{
  int value;
  Score next; // the link
} // Score

public class IntLinkedList
{
  public static void main(String[] argv) throws Exception
  {
    BufferedReader cin;
    cin = new BufferedReader(new InputStreamReader(System.in));

    // create an empty linked list
    Score start = null;

    // read and save the records
    while (true)
    {
      // create a node and read its data fields
      Score aScore = new Score();
      System.out.print("Enter a score [-1 to quit]: ");
      aScore.value = new Double(cin.readLine()).intValue();

      // check for sentinel value
      if (aScore.value == -1) break;

      // add node to front of list
      aScore.next = start;
      start = aScore;
    } // while

    // traverse the list and get the average
    int count = 0; // to count the number of nodes in the list
    int sum = 0; // to accumulate the total of all scores
    Score p;
    for (p = start; p != null; p = p.next)
    {
      sum += p.value;
      count++;
    }

    // print the result
    if (count > 0)
    {
      float average = (float)sum / count;
      System.out.print("The average of " + count + " scores is " + average);
    }
    else
      System.out.println("No values were entered.");
  } // main
} // public class
```

14.7 Exercises, Sample Code, Videos, And Addendums

Go to www.rdb3.com/java/14 for extended materials pertaining to this chapter.

Chapter 15. Some Advanced Topics

This book is an introduction to the world of computer programming. Its purpose was to turn you into a computer programmer, and if you got this far, it probably succeeded. On the later topics starting with lists (array-based and linked) only some beginning concepts were developed. For example, we did not show how to add and remove values anywhere except the end of array-based lists, and did not even mention the possibility of expanding list capacity. For linked lists we showed how to add and remove nodes at the front of a list, but did not show how to do so anywhere else, and did not deal with sorting or function calls. All of these are topics for further study in computer programming, and perhaps your study so far has inspired you to go on from here.

Before we complete our introduction, though, we want to expose you to a couple of additional programming topics: collections and recursion. They are unrelated to each other, except for the fact that they are more advanced topics in computer science. Collections, because you should not have to write array-based and linked list code the rest of your programming life. Recursion, because it is a subject that you will have to hear about more than once before you believe that it works, so we may as well start now!

15.1 The Easy Way: Collections

In modern computer languages, the details of array-based and linked list code have already been optimized by professional programmers and put into libraries for you to use. The library-defined "ArrayList" object in Java, and others like it, has library functions that implement behaviors to create lists and manage values – without the programmer having to worry about capacity or start-links and next-links. To declare an empty list of Student objects, for example, use the following:

```
ArrayList<Student> student = new ArrayList<Student>();
```

A collection is an object that can contain other objects! The required import is `import java.util.*;`.

The use of the data type **Student** enclosed in "angle brackets" in the declaration statement specifies that the list is for values of that data type. This can be used for whole number and floating point data types as well as objects, because object `class` specifications do *not* need a next-link!

To add a value to the front or end of a list, use the following:

```
              Adding A Value To A Collection
Student aStudent = new Student();
... // set the field values for aStudent

student.add(aStudent); // add at the end
                ...or...
student.add(0, aStudent); // add at the front
```

To retrieve a value from *any* position in the collection, use the following expression:

```
student.get(i)
```

`i` is an *index*, as in an array, and can be any number in the range `0` to `student.size() - 1`, inclusive. To get the value at the front, it's `student.get(0)`, and at the end, it's `student.get(student.size() - 1)`. And just like array objects, collections "know" their own size – `student.size()`. The difference is that array sizes never change – collection sizes *do* change with every `.add`.

To replace an existing value in the collection, use a statement like this:

```
student.set(i, aStudent);
```

This is not demonstrated in any code examples in this chapter, but it is included in the discussion here for completeness. Here is our code example from the previous chapter, but adapted for using collections:

Processing Student Records In A Collection [`StudentCollection.java`]

```java
import java.io.*;
import java.text.*;
import java.util.*;

class Student
{
  String name;
  int id;
  float gpa;
} // Student

public class StudentCollection
{
  static void printStudents(ArrayList<Student> student)
  {
    String blank = "                            ";
    int i;
    for (i = 0; i < student.size(); i++)
    {
      Student s = student.get(i);
      System.out.print("Name = " + s.name);
      System.out.print(blank.substring(s.name.length()));
      System.out.print(" ID = "
          + new DecimalFormat("0000000").format(s.id));
      System.out.println(" gpa = " + s.gpa);
    } // for
  } // printStudents

  public static void main(String[] argv) throws Exception
  {
    BufferedReader fin;
    fin = new BufferedReader(new FileReader("students.txt"));

    // create an empty list
    ArrayList<Student> student = new ArrayList<Student>();

    // read and save the records
    while (fin.ready())
    {
      Student aStudent = new Student();
      aStudent.name = fin.readLine();
      aStudent.id = new Double(fin.readLine()).intValue();
      aStudent.gpa = new Double(fin.readLine()).floatValue();

      fin.readLine(); // skip the separator line

      student.add(aStudent);
    } // while
    fin.close();

    printStudents(student);
  } // main
} // public class
```

215

Note that the function parameter list includes a specification for the collection.

15.2 Functions That Call Themselves: Recursion

Recursion is simply this – it's when the code block of a function contains a statement with a call to itself! This actually is a form of a loop, which would seem to be infinite. What makes it work is that the function must contain logic to decide whether to continue calling itself or not – similar to if-break in a while-true loop.

Recursion offers a new way to solve problems. If you are not using recursion, you are using "iteration" – it's what we have been using all along, but since it was the only thing we used, it really did not need a name. Iteration uses loops; recursion uses functions.

Recursion is usually an upper-level computer science topic. It is very useful in solving some types of problems, and actually *simplifies* many solutions. So if it's so simple, why is it at the end of this book, and why is it upper-level? That's because it is difficult for most people to understand right away – even people with strong aptitudes for computers. This is something that you will have to hear now and believe later!

To apply recursion, you just need to know these things about the problem you are solving: (1) how to solve a base case, and (2) how to reduce problem complexity towards a base case. Then you need to be able to divide problems into two parts: (1) the part you know how to solve, and (2) the part you don't know how to solve.

15.2.1 Simple Example: Countdown
This ridiculously easy example demonstrates the sequence for developing a recursive solution. The problem is this: NASA has hired you to write a countdown program, starting from any non-negative whole number and ending at zero. (NASA uses this kind of thing a lot, and they want to automate it!) You first consider using an *iterative* solution, but you soon conclude that it is just

too difficult (work with me here...). So you next consider using a *recursive* solution instead.

The problem, then, is this: count down from the `int` variable `n`. First, write down the part you know how to do: say the number stored in `n`. Then write down the part you don't know how to do: count down from `n` minus one. For example, if `n` is "10", the recursive solution is to say "10", and then count down from "9". If you wrote a function to do this, and the number to count down from is in the parameter list, the body of the function would do these two things: output the variable from the parameter list, and then call a function that knows how to count down from that value minus one. And here's the tricky part – the function we would call to do that is the function we are currently writing! Seems a bit like the chicken-and-the-egg dilemma, doesn't it.

The only problem that remains is to identify a "base case", and use that in a logic statement to stop the recursion. The base case is this: if we were asked to count down from zero, it would be easy – just say "0"! In that case, if the value of the variable in the parameter list is zero, no additional call needs to be made.

Here is the full solution (which you are free to copy, modify, and share with NASA – you're welcome):

```
                Recursive Countdown [CountDown.java]

import java.io.*;

public class CountDown
{
  static void countDown(int n)
  {
    System.out.print("" + n + ' '); // the part I know how to do
    if (n > 0) // look for base case
      countDown(n - 1); // do this if not base case
  } // countDown

  public static void main(String[] argv) throws Exception
  {
    BufferedReader cin;
    cin = new BufferedReader(new InputStreamReader(System.in));

    int n;
    System.out.print("Enter n: ");
    n = new Double(cin.readLine()).intValue();

    countDown(n);
    System.out.println();
  } // main
} // public class
```

15.2.2 Classic Example: Factorial
The classic introductory example for recursion is factorial. In math class you may have seen a symbol like this: **5!**, pronounced "five factorial". It is the equivalent of 5 x 4 x 3 x 2 x 1, or 120. Factorials show up in probability calculations for such things as lotteries.

The problem is this: we want a function to calculate the factorial of a non-negative number, **n**. First we consider coming up with an iterative solution, and we quickly decide that it is too complicated (again, work with me here). So we consider using recursion. First, there is a base case: **0!** is defined as 1 – actually, **1!** is also 1 – both are base cases. Working towards the base case, **n!** is **n** (the part we know how to solve) times **(n-1)!** (the part we do not know how to solve). Luckily we have a function to solve the latter – the function we are writing! So the recursive solution is **n! = n x (n-1)!**:

The Classic Recursive Factorial [Factorial.java]

```
import java.io.*;

public class Factorial
{
  static int factorial(int n)
  {
    int result;
    if (n < 2) // detect a base case
      result = 1;
    else
      result = n * factorial(n - 1);
    return result;
  } // factorial

  public static void main(String[] argv) throws Exception
  {
    BufferedReader cin;
    cin = new BufferedReader(new InputStreamReader(System.in));

    int n;
    System.out.print("Enter n: ");
    n = new Double(cin.readLine()).intValue();

    System.out.println(factorial(n));
  } // main
} // public class
```

15.2.3 A Caution...

Do not get too attached to recursion. There is always an iterative solution to everything – it's just that recursion is sometimes simpler to code, once you get familiar enough with it. But recursion is usually less efficient than iteration, so use iteration if you can. Use recursion as a convenience, realizing that there is a cost involved. And sometimes that cost is too much, even for the easiest of recursive solutions – try counting down from 100000 and see! If that works, then try a million...

15.3 Where Do We Go From Here?

This introduction to programming used Java to make the concepts real. These concepts, such as variables, code blocks, branching and looping logic, subprograms, arrays, and lists, are common to all programming languages. What you learned here actually serves as the introduction that you would need to go on to the study of *any* specific language – not just Java.

If this is where you end your study of programming, then hopefully you found this interesting and enlightening, and you have a better understanding of how computers work and what computer programming professionals do. If this is just the beginning for you, then you are ready to master one or more languages and then learn techniques of problem solving. You will likely eventually learn to develop user interfaces and write GUI (graphical user interface) programs. You may learn to be a solo programmer or a member of a team of programmers. You may write scientific simulations, business databases, or interactive games. Whatever you do, it's a great profession with an unlimited future, and you will always be glad you found your way into it!

Appendix: The Java Library

Here is a compilation of all the identifiers from the Java library, which are used in this book. The table below lists examples of expressions and the library that needs to be imported in order to use the expression. Note that some do not require an import statement, because they are in the `java.lang` library, which is automatically imported. Also, some do require that `throws Exception` be appended to `main`, and to any other subprograms that use them.

expression example	import library	needs throws Exception
`Arrays.sort(...);`	java.util	no
`Character.toLowerCase(char)`	none	no
`Character.toUpperCase(char)`	none	no
`Math.abs(numeric value)`	none	no
`Math.cos(numeric value)`	none	no
`Math.exp(numeric value)`	none	no
`Math.pow(numeric value, numeric value)`	none	no
`Math.random()`	none	no
`Math.sin(numeric value)`	none	no
`Math.sqrt(numeric value)`	none	no
`new ArrayList()`	java.util	no
`new BufferedReader(new FileReader(String))`	java.io	yes
`new BufferedReader(new InputStreamReader(System.in))`	java.io	yes
`new DecimalFormat("#.00").format(double));`	java.text	no
`new Double(...)`	none	no
`new PrintWriter(new FileWriter(String))`	java.io	yes
`Thread.sleep(int)`	none	yes

Index

Symbols

&& 77
|| 78

A

append 150, 157, 177
array 163, 169
    as function parameter 177
    element 133, 165, 167, 168,
        169, 170, 171, 175
    index 165
    searching 169
    size 167
    sorting 171, 174
    traversal 167
array-based list 191, 209
ArrayList 213
Arrays.sort 174
assignment
    statement 46, 48
    upon declaration 45

B

backup 32
boolean 143, 145
Boolean 143
branching 21, 22, 73, 81, 94, 204,
    219
break 97, 98
byte 137, 138, 142, 143

C

calculation 21, 22, 42, 45, 47, 48,
    58, 59, 61, 65
case 16, 42, 58
casting 145
cin.readLine() 68
classic solutions 91, 105, 134
cloud folder 31
code block 27, 62
collections 213
comments 59, 85
compiler 15, 18, 25, 28, 29, 40,
    59, 156, 184
    command line 37
    error 156
complex expressions 49
computer memory 136
continue 91
convention 42, 58, 192, 205
count-controlled 98
curly-brace container 35, 44, 83
curly-brace initialization 168, 175
cycle 81, 89, 91, 111, 141, 208

D

DecimalFormat 61, 62, 141
declaration statement 43
DeMorgan's Theorem 120
design considerations 179, 184
dot operator 186
do-while loop 88

E

echo 61
editor 15, 16, 17, 18, 25, 27, 34,
    35, 40, 90, 149, 154
else-if logic 94, 96
end-of-file loop 152
entry point 20
event-controlled 98
expression 7, 19, 53, 60, 221

F

flash drive 27, 31, 32
floating point numbers 140
for-loop 103, 104
formatting output 60
function 23
    call 122
    definition 122

H

hide extensions 33

I

identifiers 42, 46, 57, 125, 184,
    221
if-break 83, 94, 98, 99, 115, 152,
    153, 216
if-else logic 79
if-statement 73, 74, 76, 79, 80, 81,
    94, 97, 114, 173
if-Statement 73, 113
infinite loops 83, 85
infinity 138
input 5, 6, 7, 15, 65, 126, 153, 176,
    180
integer division 59

J

Java
    JDK 27
    JRE 27
java.io 66
java.math 58
java.se 30
java.text 60
java.util 174
JNotePad 17, 27, 35

L

labels 54
length() 51, 57, 159, 168, 173, 186,
    187, 202
line breaks 27
line wrap 90
linked lists 8, 204, 211
    node 205, 206
    removing a node 206
    start-link 205
    traversal 208
Linux 7, 17, 25, 27, 28, 34
list
    capacity 192, 195, 196, 204,
    213
literal value 144
logic 40, 77, 79, 92, 94, 95, 96,
    111, 119, 120, 134, 152, 153,
    158, 216, 217, 219
looping 21
lowercase 16, 42, 58, 79, 84, 118,
    119, 145, 173, 202

M

Mac 17, 25, 26, 27, 31, 32, 34, 35
Math.pow 57

method 23
min/max logic 91, 105, 134
mixed case 118

N

negative numbers 43
negative Numbers 138
nested loop 107
NotePad
  PC 17
not operator 120

O

object 7, 66, 148, 153, 183, 185,
  188
  array 187
  declaration 185
  specification 183, 184, 204
Object 205
object-oriented programming 7,
  189
operand 47
output 5, 7, 15, 52, 53

P

parameter lists 126, 177
pass by reference 177, 188
Pass By Reference 181, 182
pass by value 177
PC 25, 27, 31, 32, 35
precision 43, 44, 136, 140, 141
prompt 65, 67, 68, 150

Q

quiz program 86

R

randomizing 130

range limitations 138, 139
recursion 8, 213, 216, 217, 218,
  219
Recursion 213, 216
return statement 126
reverse logic 119

S

scope 89, 121, 180
searching 169, 195
sentinel 84, 105, 106, 107
sequential processing 19, 20, 22,
  46, 48, 83, 122, 123, 124, 127,
  148
sleep 111
sorting 92, 134, 171, 174, 195
source file 35, 36, 38
source files 32
statement 7, 19, 221
subprogram 22, 23, 180
switch-statement 96

T

temporary variable 181
TextEdit 17, 25, 26, 27, 34, 35
text file input 147
text file output 153
traversing 208
truncation 59
type casting. See casting

U

UNIX 7, 17, 25, 34
unpredictable 101, 168, 173
uppercase 16, 42, 79, 84, 145, 173,
  192, 202

V

validation loop 89, 122
value 40, 68, 205
variable 41, 53, 60, 175
    uninitialized 52

W

while-true-if-break 83, 94
while-true loop 81, 83, 87
word wrap 26
working folder 31, 32, 35, 36, 149,
    154

Made in the USA
Lexington, KY
06 July 2017